MAKE MONEY YOUR B!TCH

A WOMAN'S ROADMAP TO FINANCIAL FREEDOM

AMBER PARR & KATHERINE HAYES

First published by Ultimate World Publishing 2020
Copyright © 2020 Amber Parr & Katherine Hayes

ISBN

Paperback - 978-1-925884-94-4
Ebook - 978-1-925884-95-1

Cover design: Ultimate World Publishing
Layout and typesetting: Ultimate World Publishing
Editor: Rusti L Lehay

ULTIMATE WORLD
— PUBLISHING —

Ultimate World Publishing
Diamond Creek,
Victoria Australia 3089
www.writeabook.com.au

CONTENTS

$ $ $

Disclaimer

The authors of this book have written this book based on their own experiences and learnings and offer their stories for your enjoyment and to guide you in your own learning. The intent of the authors is to offer information that is general in nature and this information does not take into account your individual financial situation or personal circumstances. In the event that you use any of the information in this book for yourself, the authors and publisher assume no responsibility for your actions.

DEDICATION

$ $ $

To Peter - Thank you for wisdom and helping us to aim higher.

INTRODUCTION

— $ $ $ —

Money for many of us is an awkward subject to talk about. It's wrapped up in our childhood experiences and subconscious beliefs. For some people it is full of fear or shame. For others, it is synonymous with privilege and status. No matter what thoughts or feelings the word 'money' brings to mind, the truth is we all need it and use it everyday. So it's somewhat surprising that for something so essential and at times controversial, financial literacy levels are generally pretty low. Some people reach adulthood not really knowing or maybe even barely knowing anything about money apart from the balance of their monthly credit card statement (if they are brave enough to look.) Money management and financial education isn't something we are taught in school, so we are left to figure it out on our own. So well done you. Buying a book about money (and reading it) actually puts you ahead of the curve. And if you are a woman, statistically, you need all the help you can get.

In Australia, on average, a woman will retire with over $90,000 less in her superannuation than her male counterparts. This is despite the fact that women make up nearly half of the workforce. But almost half of those employed women work part-time (compared with one in six men). The gender pay-gap is real and can affect women throughout their working lives which also has a direct impact on their retirement savings. No one should aim to retire and live off the age pension alone. Based on the rates for 2019, if you are single and receiving the age pension, you will receive $466 a week. A WEEK!!!!! That means food, utilities, rent or rates, fuel, car registration... the works. The pension is not a right or entitlement for a lifetime of paying taxes, it's a welfare safety-net for those with no other options.

Let's not aim for that. **Let's aim higher.** To have a comfortable self-funded retirement, complete with extravagant holidays or something new and special for you or loved ones, just because it's a Tuesday in July. **Let's aim for enough to save, share and spend, free of constraints.**

There is an increasing number of women hitting retirement age with insufficient funds to support themselves. These are women who have worked for most of their lives. It's a terrifying reality for far too many.

It's a sad fact that women are more often than not, at a financial disadvantage compared to our male peers. This book was born out of a desire to turn that around. This book is not just about retirement. The take-aways can be used by both genders. *Make Money your Bitch* is about being able to pay your bills, take holidays with your kids or finally do that thing that you always wanted to do. It's about having the freedom to do the things that will enrich your life, which will look different for you than it does for someone else. Our intention is for you to feel as though money no longer controls you, but instead becomes a tool that fits perfectly in your hands. After this book, you will be able to handle this tool with precision and craft a life that is perfect for you. Once again, our goal in writing this book for you:

Money no longer controls you;
Money is a tool that fits perfectly in your hands.
You handle this tool with Precision.
Crafting a life perfect for you.

If you are single, it's time to really understand where you are financially and make a plan for where you want to be. If you are in a committed relationship and your finances are combined with your other half, (not all couples run their money like this) it's time to help steer the financial ship. Maybe a generation ago it was common for the men to run the budget alone. Today, partners should have equal say in the household budget (regardless of who earns what).

This is not a trivial matter. Sadly, a large percentage of marriage breakdowns occur as a result of arguing over money matters and financial stress. There's even a name for it now, 'financial infidelity'. We think we can safely say that all kinds of 'infidelity' are bad for relationships. Getting on the same page financially with your significant other is an essential ingredient in having a long term, happy partnership.

Financial security is something everyone wants to achieve, but it's a little bit like getting fit. It doesn't just happen because you agree it's a good idea and can see the benefits. There is work to do. You not only need to know what to do, you need to start doing it and keep doing it.

Throughout the following chapters we will give you the 'how to' guide. We also have an online community so you can share your journey with others like you.

We have stories of tough financial times, whether it is living off rice and sweet chilli sauce because that's all the budget could afford or hanging out at friend's house until it became uncomfortably awkward and late into the evening to the point where a friend felt they HAD to extend an invite to stay for dinner. Or filling up a car with EXACTLY five dollars in fuel to get to work and home. Honestly, these now make hilarious anecdotes and sometimes when retelling them, we start them with, "In my day..."

But those days are over for us and here at Money Madams, we want them to be over for you too.

Everyone knows that money does not make you happy. But being poor sure does suck arse. Money in and of itself is just a thing. It's not good or bad. It is just a means to give you options.

Imagine... taking that job you like in a new city that pays less but makes your heart soar? -buying that house you really want and smashing out your mortgage? -taking extended parental leave? -or a sabbatical to travel? It's all about prioritising and creating the life you want to lead on your terms and feeling in control.

Did you see your parents struggle with money issues, without real solutions? Was 'money' a topic of conversation that was instantly 'hot'. Or, was it 'handle' with silence?

Maybe you've grown up watching your parents struggle financially and don't want to make the same mistakes yourself. Perhaps money is a mystery to you and you want to make sure you aren't a slave to your finances. Whatever your reason for picking up this book, we are glad you did and we are here to guide you on your money journey with some good advice and a sense of humour, because let's face it, very few people enjoy talking about money, let alone reading about money.

This book is not a get rich quick scheme. It is not about making your first million before you're thirty or having a private jet. It's about empowering women so they can make good decisions and reach their goals. *God that sounds boring.* It's like your mum making you eat all your vegetables. But hey, maybe mum was onto something.

CHAPTER 1

GET IT TOGETHER

$ $ $

So, when you feel like there is so much to tackle, where do you start? At the beginning of course, and that means discussing the dreaded "B" word. Your budget.

What do you think about when you hear the word 'budget'? Do you shudder? Do you think about past attempts where the reality never quite reconciled with your intentions? No one likes to think about a budget. In fact, even the word is offensive. It's like the word 'diet'. It brings up feelings of having less than you need. Going on a money diet. Yuck. It sounds like you would end up hungry and broke. Let's banish that word altogether. In this chapter we are going to talk about a 'Spending Plan.' There, we feel better about this already.

**Take the word 'budget' out of your money vocabulary.
Replace it with 'Spending Plan'.**

Wouldn't life be much easier if we could all just spend money on whatever we wanted, whenever we wanted..... YES!!!! Unfortunately, this is not the reality for the vast majority of us. We all need a Spending Plan. But this doesn't have to involve feelings of pain and self-deprivation.

It is essentially about priorities. Of course you will need to make sure that you have enough money to cover the essentials. Things like paying the rent or mortgage, food, utilities and making sure you have money set aside for transport. But it is NOT about excluding yourself from spending money on the things you enjoy or giving up on having fun. It's about making sure you can live within your means – so you can have fun and enjoy what makes YOU happy. It's about being conscious with how you spend your money. We can all fall into habits and routines with our finances that don't serve us in the long run. We need to take some time to consider what we genuinely need, what we enjoy and what's important to us.

Here is one of Amber's own examples: *"What I realised a little while ago was that I was in a habit of buying a certain bottle of wine. I liked the wine but honestly I can feel a little intimidated when I go into the bottle shop, so I would just buy the one I knew. It wasn't super expensive and I could afford it. But one night a friend came over to my place and brought a bottle of wine with her. I enjoyed the wine she brought and told her so. She said it was one of her favourites too but also that it was cheap. She told me the wine was less than half the price of the wine I liked. I had to ask myself, did I enjoy my usual wine more than double the amount that I enjoyed her bottle? Nope, I didn't."*

Expensive wine is not a priority for either of us. Instead, we both like to travel and have memorable experiences. What really brings us joy is the adventure of exploring new places and trying new things. So that's our priority; it's what we like spending our money on. Even if it's just a weekend away. Spending time doing something out of the ordinary with family or friends, brings both of us real joy. Much more than a fancy bottle of wine. But that's just us. It will be different for everyone. Take some time to think about what you spend your money on.

Mini Quiz:

- What do you spend your money on?
- Do you really enjoy those things?
- How long does that feeling last?
- Does it replenish you?
- Excite you? Energise you?
- Refresh you?
- Do you look forward to it?

Okay, so if you were a client coming to sit down and meet to talk about your financial future, what would I tell you? The first thing is that you need to create a good, old-fashioned budget (how has that horrible word crept in again?). We meant, Spending Plan! Yes, it is a spin-off of the old budget with a twist. A budget gives off a sense of 'limitation', while Spending Plan, gives us a sense of Money Management and is a living document. We like to use the terms Living Budget and Spending Plan interchangeably. The difference between a budget and a Spending Plan is more important than just semantics. For most people, a budget will fail them. That's why people hate it so much and that's why we think a Spending Plan is a much better idea.

How many times have you eagerly prepared a budget thinking you are going to change your life, then only two days later forget all about it, or find yourself wondering why you don't have as much money left over as your budget indicated you should have? Do you feel like a failure or feel ashamed? Do you feel that it's just all too hard? That maybe you are just not smart enough?

Well, we're here to tell you that it's easy, even if you never had any good examples or teachings on smart money management, you can gain the smarts now. Our method, once implemented, will barely take up any of your time. Does that sound good? You betcha it does!

The trick is to make a *Living* Budget. A run-of-the-mill budget tells you what you should spend, a Living Budget helps to automate your cash-flow by putting some controls in place so you don't have to constantly check in with a spreadsheet. If you automate your budget, you'll barely have to think about it. **It will become a full-fledged Spending Plan.**

Don't get me wrong, a budget is a handy tool, but unless you use it well and take it to the next level, it'll be nothing more than a great idea. There are a lot of great apps out there that can help you track your spending, but many of these simply tell you what you've done, and if you go over, it's mostly a rearward looking exercise. A big slap in the face that says better luck next time!

So yes, you still need one, but we want you to have a "Living" Budget that automates your cash flow and spending, so you don't have to look at your budget constantly.

The Trick is:
Create your Spending Plan, your Living Budget.
Then Automate it...
So it mostly takes care of itself.

Lucky for you we have a tool to help you do exactly that. We have a Money Madams Living Budget template which is designed to help you set up your Spending Plan. If this is of interest to you, jump on our website and check it out, we've saved you all the hard work!

So how should you allocate your pay packet?

The first thing we're going to tell you to do is to start setting aside money for any big picture goals. Whatever your big picture or dream is, if it's important, treat it as a priority.

Most people save what's left, but that's why they never have any money left to save as it's on the bottom of their priority list. If you've already completed your Spending Plan and you don't have anything to spare, you have a problem. A big problem. You need to cut some expenses out of your Spending Plan or increase your income by getting yourself a pay raise or side hustle. Whatever your take-home pay is, you should aim to save 10%, preferably more. If you can save more, fabulous, if you can't do this right now, start small and work towards it.

So why is saving for bigger picture items so important? This is the money that literally changes your life. This is what ticks your boxes in life whether it's a home deposit, retiring in comfort, or investing so instead of you working for money, money works for you. This is the money that takes you from where you are now, to wherever you want to be. In short, it sets you up for anything you want in your own Big Picture down the track.

Next we are going to break down the money you spend over the course of the year into 4 categories.

The first step is to separate your needs (food, fuel and shelter, et cetera) from your wants (any personal luxuries such as bought lunches or entertainment). This gives you the first two categories. What about the other two? Now I want you to divide your needs and wants into your spending timeframes now (monthly or less often) or later (anything paid less often)

So your four areas are as follows: **Needs Now, Needs Later, Wants Now** and you guessed it, **Wants Later**. But those names are pretty boring. So we've made them a little more descriptive and used simple names for each category.

A popular method to break up your pay packet used to be physically dividing your paycheck into separate cash envelopes to cover your various expenses, but in today's fast-paced lifestyle where most things are paid for electronically, this is no longer realistically feasible. I rarely carry more than $50 in cash on me for fear of losing it, let alone can even contemplate the idea of dropping a neat $1,000 at my local post office to pay a stack of bills. I'd be so terrified of losing the money, that I'd likely stuff my cash in a combination of my purse, pockets or down my bra. By the time I got to the counter I'd look like a stripper pulling out her tips from the night before. No thanks, I think I'll stick to internet banking!

So instead of using envelopes to store cash. Take the same approach and do it with your bank accounts. Your 4 categories and account names are mapped out below.

Let's get a quick overview of each category, so you can get this right.

```
                          NOW

         "Splurge"          |    "Everyday Expenses"
                            |
                            |
WANT ───────────────────────────────────────── NEED
                            |
         "Future Fun"       |        "Big Bills"
                            |

                         LATER
```

So what kind of expenses should go into each category?

Everyday expenses: This is for the necessities, expenses or services and items that would be difficult to live without. Most of these bills are pretty consistent each month and can be direct debited straight from this account such as your phone, internet, rent or mortgage repayments etc. This is your main account and doubles up as your cash hub.

Fun Fact: Did you know that internet access is now rated as being just as essential as food, shelter and water by Gen Y's in a recent study... back in my day... never mind, let's move on.

But what about variable expenses such as groceries and fuel? These are funded from the same account, but these are the only two items under this method that you can't direct debit. You need to whip out your debit card. These are the only two expenses you would need to pay attention to. While you can't control fuel prices, you can be mindful of taking any unnecessary trips, and choose where you shop and what kind of food you buy. Once you settle an amount you plan to spend on these items, stick to it.

Now just because you have a regular bill, it doesn't mean it automatically fits into this category, remember the golden rule, it has to be difficult to live without. Things like entertainment subscriptions (Netflix, Foxtel & Spotify etc) and gym memberships are all great to have and enjoyable, but at the end of the day aren't essential. You can include them here as a shared expense if you're a couple, but just remember if your Spending Plan is overcommitted, these are the first items on the chopping block.

If you have an ambitious savings goal, avoid these subscription services. If you have them already, you can sometimes suspend them for a period of time, while you focus on something like paying down debt or reaching your savings goal. No one likes to say no to things they enjoy but having a clear plan makes this easier, especially if it's only for a limited time or you need an intensive burst of savings to get you ahead or out of a rut, but cutting back indefinitely isn't sustainable and this is where it can become too hard and you may feel like you want to give up. So if your Spending Plan allows you to go to the gym, watch Netflix etc, while still being able to save, do it. Include the things that ease your life and bring you joy and value.

Big Bills: Once you've got your day-to-day necessities under control, it's time to sort out your longer-term necessities or as we like to call them your "Big bills." The only difference here from your everyday expenses is how frequently you typically have to pay these bills. These are bills that you would generally pay each quarter, each year or perhaps even less often. Go through and itemise all of the Big Bills that you incur each year that are essential. Items such as utilities (gas, water and electricity), car registration and vehicle servicing costs or any bills where paying annually would give you a worthwhile discount such as insurances.

Don't forget to include ad hoc expenses that don't have a specific due date each year, such as tyres for your car, replacing a pair of glasses, trips to the dentist or other medical appointments including those for your pets.

Whatever the total is... Add a buffer of 10%, because these bills have a nasty way of increasing suddenly and unexpectedly from time to time. Just whip out your calculator, enter the annual total and times it by 1.1.

When these bills come in, the aim is that you'll already have the money ready to go, and it will have no impact on your day to day cashflow. No more nasty bill shocks for you!

To make this strategy work, you will need to have an initial buffer in this account. There's no point kicking off this strategy a month before your car registration and insurance renewal is due, you will need a small float or buffer to get it working smoothly. To get your Big Bills account up and running, direct your 10% savings buffer into this account until you have a buffer. Otherwise you can sell some unwanted items around your home, pick up extra hours, or if you are expecting a juicy tax refund or bonus, get this sorted. Once that's done, the regular transfer after each pay from your Everyday Expenses account into your Big Bills account will mean you'll always be prepared!

Splurge: This is quite simple. It's the things that you CAN live without, but you wouldn't want to because it's what makes your life more enjoyable. The things you want now. These are the things that you look forward to, that make you happy. Most people exclude these when they are making a budget and that's what makes it hard and unsustainable. This category is personal to you. We'll give you a hint, coffees and smashed avocado at your local cafe, go here. We fully support you in making sure you get to enjoy all your hard work whether it's a daily luxury like a coffee or enjoying yourself out and about.

This is the money you are allowed to enjoy entirely guilt-free. This category is especially important for couples, because this is an argument-free territory. No criticism or judgement allowed. If you hate the idea of making lunch at home and taking it to work and want to buy lunch from a local café go for it. If you like to fork out for the latest fashion or tech accessory, go nuts. If you have an expensive hobby that you love to indulge in and life would be boring or meaningless without it, you guessed it... it all gets accounted for here.

Planning your spending around the things you want and not going over can be really difficult for many people to manage, but we are going to give you a short and simple set of rules to make it fail proof.

1. Have a dedicated bank account for your splurge money.
2. This account is yours and yours alone, do NOT make this a joint account.
3. Pay yourself weekly regardless of how often you actually get paid.
4. When the money is gone, that's it! Credit cards are off limits.

So why does this work?

Most people have money hang-ups. (Who doesn't?!) If you are reading this, you're probably one of them.

The 'Splurge' allocation in your Spending Plan is yours to enjoy guilt-free.

I know we have already said that, but that's because it's important. Seriously, there are no judgements here. This is your permission to be kind to you and enjoy it in the way that you will get the most enjoyment from it. So if you like buying lunch each day, go for it. If you don't touch your money most days, but you want to splash out every other weekend or get your hair and lashes done every 6 weeks, that's okay, there is no requirement for you to spend all your money, but the simple rule is that when it's gone, it's gone. The benefit of paying yourself weekly is that if you burn through your money in a few days, well it's really only a few days before you get paid again. You CAN handle a few days without spending money, if your basic needs are being met.

The reason you have a separate bank account is that you owe no one an explanation or justification as to how and why you spend this money on the things you want. It's judgement-free territory, and sometimes it's just nice to be able to surprise your partner with a gift without the surprise being spoiled when they look at a joint account statement or see the transaction history in your internet banking. You also aren't allowed to criticise your partner either. The 'no-judgement rule' is a two way street. Many couples end up referring to these accounts as 'marriage money'. Couples who set up their finances this way no longer find themselves eyeing off each other's purchases. They feel safe in the knowledge they are both committed to the household finances because they have freedom to spend money independently as they see fit without it detracting from their common goals. Imagine if you and your partner no longer argued about money!!

Paying yourself an allowance is ESSENTIAL.
Your willpower is not infinite.
You've got to be able to let loose, but within defined limits.
There is a lot to be said for freedom within limits.

If you don't give yourself a little bit of monetary freedom, you'll feel constrained, and you will overspend and that's when feelings of shame and failure start to creep in. So even if you can initially only afford to set aside enough money to enjoy a cup of coffee with a friend from time to time, make sure you do it.

When you are working hard, and all your money is going to pay the bills, it can get quite depressing pretty quickly. That's why it's vital to make sure you have regular spending money just for you. This might not be a tremendous amount at certain stages in your life, so take time to consider the things that make you happy. Is it catching up for coffee or lunch with friends, is it having the latest fashion or gadgets? Whatever it is, do it and enjoy it. Make sure you celebrate and spend it on the things you value, and that bring you joy. Just make sure you set yourself a fixed amount and stick to it. This may mean you have to scale back initially if you're not saving as much as you'd like, the key is to set a limit, and never go over it.

Of course, there is no requirement for you to spend all your splurge money. I (Katherine) spend a small amount of my spending allocation on coffee each week, and when I'm disorganised, takeaway lunches. But for the most part, I'm usually pretty good at spending less than what I set aside for myself each week, and this allows me to splurge on more significant expenses such as a weekend away or going on a shopping spree when my favourite stores are on sale and I need a serious wardrobe update. *Amber on the other hand spends every cent of her spending money, every week on coffees and lunches and dinners and things that she has nothing to show for at the end of the week. But she is the extrovert and loves catching up with friends and has a great time doing it. (Pick which one is the financial adviser...)*

Future Fun: That leaves your last account. Your longer-term wants. We're confident you are getting the idea now. These are the special things we celebrate or enjoy that happen consistently each year that require money to be set aside so you can fully enjoy it free of financial stress or guilt that could otherwise derail your enjoyment of the event.

We are talking about saving up for annual holidays, and setting aside money for special events such as Christmas, birthdays and anniversary dinners.

You have to keep this money separate from your day-to-day spending otherwise you'll spend it, and there will never be enough! These are important to include because these are the things we remember fondly and are experiences that often form the basis of our special memories when we look back in later years.

A wise man once told me that we have a responsibility to create memories, because there may come a time in our lives when it is all we have left.

Whether it's because a special person in our life has moved on, or because we lose our health and reflecting on those memories can be what keeps us going. Travel and special occasions are great ways to create some of these memories.

But what if your Spending Plan is so tight that setting aside money for these events is extremely difficult and you start to feel guilty or inadequate believing that you are somehow depriving yourself or your children of memorable experiences? Special moments can be as simple as doing something ordinary in an unordinary way or creating your own unique family traditions.

I know one family that had a hectic work schedule and they made a tradition of having their Friday night dinners as a picnic tent under their dining table. A friend of ours introduced us to the red plate tradition.

Whenever someone did something above or beyond or reached a milestone, they were served dinner on the prestigious red plate and their achievement was proudly announced to all family members.

Amber loves to host Easter gatherings where the grown-ups get to drink champagne out of hollow chocolate Easter bunnies, while the children drink chocolate milk out of theirs (her tip is to do this outside because to her utter surprise some chocolate Easter bunnies are not structurally sound. Who knew?). In my family, we celebrate Dinovember each year (go on, you know you want to google it) and at the end of the year we order dinner plates which displays all of our kids favourite artworks from the school year.

So whether you are splash with your cash or feeling the pinch, make moments that count.

I need to point out that these accounts are not for saving up for one-off big-ticket items like a home deposit, these accounts are about setting aside money with the intention of spending it on something you want each year so you don't feel caught out in these moments. If you have a specific goal that will take more than a year such as saving up for a car or a home deposit, use a high interest savings account specifically for whatever your goals are, and don't withdraw from this account for any purpose other than that specific goal. These goals are for your big picture accounts and you can have as many goals as you want or need.

Setting up your transfers

When you get paid, where should your pay go? We like to use the Everyday Expenses account as the central cash hub for all money that comes in whether it's your paycheck, investments, rental income or government rebates or benefits. In short all money coming in goes into the one account. If you are a couple in a committed relationship, this is a joint household account and both of your pays go here.

Access the Money Madams spending plan template at www.moneymadams.com/shop .

Next, work out how much to transfer from your Everyday expenses account into your "Big Bills" and "Future Fund" accounts. If you are using the Money Madams Living Budget Template, this will be worked out for you automatically. If not, all you need to do is divide your total by how many pays you receive in a year. E.g. monthly = 12, fortnightly = 26 and weekly = 52.

Then schedule automatic transfers for that amount from your Everyday Expenses account to your "Big Bills" and "Future Fund" accounts for the day after each payday. Or better yet, get your employer to divide your pay up for you. Note: if you are using an e-saver or internet saver account this option may not be available so you may need to go with the first option of setting up the automatic transfers yourself.

So what if you get paid monthly? Or you and your partner are on different pay frequencies? These categories will still work, and what's even better, will help to smooth out the up and down bumps in your cashflow by taking out the massive highs and lows. In our house we find it is easier to line up the transfers to the pay period of whoever has the biggest pay packet. In short choose the frequency that works for your household, you may line up the Big Bills with one person's pay day, and your Future Fund to the other person's pay packet. Do what works for you.

When it comes to your 'Splurge' account, set up an automatic transfer to yourself for the same day each week to be transferred from your 'Everyday Expenses' account across to your 'Splurge' account each week, regardless of your pay frequency. One of the keys to making sure you stick to your Splurge Spending Plan is to pay yourself each and every week. We are big fans of paying yourself on a Thursday so you have cash for the weekend.

If you find that you've spent the whole lot by the time you go to work on Monday, it will only be a matter of days before you get your next hit, and there's probably less likelihood that you'll be hitting the stores during your work week. If you don't work the typical Monday to Friday, choose a day of the week that suits you and your spending patterns.

You have now automated your Living Budget!

You now know how much is required for each of your 4 categories each month. It doesn't matter whether you get paid, weekly, fortnightly or monthly, all you need to do is make sure you have set up automatic transfers from your Everyday expenses account to the other 3 categories. Your budget is now coming to life! You have a Living Budget.

You budget is now highly automated. The only thing you need to watch is your card usage. For anything personal it's limited to the cash available in your individual splurge account.

For your Everyday expenses account, your rent or loan repayments, and monthly bills are all being direct debited. To make sure you stay within your Spending Plan limit for this account, the only area you have to track is when you pull out your debit card to pay for your grocery spend and fuel each month. How easy is that!

For this you can use an app. I'm a fan of ASIC 's MoneySmart's track-my-spend app. It's free and it doesn't require you to provide third party access to your bank accounts.

Now there is only one more step to make sure that your new Spending Plan is a success...

To make your Spending Plan, Your Living Budget a complete success, there's one more step.

Plan a Review

One thing is constant, and that's change. Whether it's the general cost of living going up, changes to your work arrangements, interest rates on loans, yep, it's gonna change.

Another reason to book in a review of your Spending Plan is that the first time you give this a go, you may discover after a while that there is something you missed or maybe you over or underestimated some of your expenses. My favourite time to review my Living Budget is roughly every 6 months when I get my winter-gas heating bill or my summer-cooling electricity bill. These bills previously freaked me out, but now I find myself calm and in control knowing I have the money set aside and it's a timely reminder to make sure that these expenses are still in line with my estimates.

If you find there are times where you are pulling out your debit card for household expenses that aren't in your Spending Plan, use something like the MoneySmart track-my-spend app mentioned above. This is a way of seeing where your Spending Plan may need updating because you may have missed an expense.

For me this was stores like Kmart and Target when I would often purchase clothes and shoes for my kids, or household items. I hate storing paper receipts and often couldn't remember exactly what I purchased, so noting it down at the time helped me get a good idea of how much I needed to set aside for these expenses over a period of time and include it in my Living Budget. It also meant that if I had a second trip to a similar store, I could see how much I had already spent that month.

On a final Living Budget note: Change your direct debits.

A big part of this exercise may mean having to change your direct debits. I'm an all-out budgeting nerd, but even for me, this last part can feel like a tiresome exercise, but it's where the plan comes to life and is also a great way to confirm what expenses you have going on and a solid opportunity to take the time to think about whether or not the expense is worth continuing to include in your Spending Plan moving forward.

If you can, find a way to make it fun (margaritas & nachos!!), or better yet, find a friend who you know wants to get her shit together and make each other accountable and learn to get comfortable talking about money as you both share your wins and successes!

What if my partner and I struggle to agree on our spending goals and priorities?

This is a tough one. If you have joint finances, it is important to be on the same page as each other when it comes to your household goals. Amber often jokes that when it comes to walking down the aisle or watching a fairytale ending in a movie, the line "...they lived forever happily ever after...," should in reality be replaced with "...and they compromised for evermore..." In all seriousness, being in a relationship means having give and take on both sides. This requires having a good conversation with your partner about making sure that you're sharing the same journey together. Talking about your finances should be something that you do on a regular basis, so you can both be accountable to each other.

If you can't agree about money and it's causing relationship difficulties, then it's probably worthwhile seeing a counsellor or psychologist to understand how your values may differ. Now this is entirely different to somebody that has an addiction, for example such as gambling, or other expenses that are unhealthy for the family finances or go beyond a reasonable level. Once again, if how each of you handles money and budgeting is causing an issue for your finances and is putting you and your family under financial stress, we urge you to seek professional help.

CHAPTER 2

GET BACK UP

— $ $ $ —

You don't have to be a grown up for long to realise that life doesn't usually go to plan. Shit happens (and happens often). Your car can break down (on the rainiest night), your washing machine will die (mid-gastro outbreak) or your kid could do a cartwheel and have their brand-new glasses fall off onto the cement just in time for another kid to run past, slide on the glasses and scratch the crap out of them (ok, maybe the last one is just Amber's kid).

What we are saying is that we don't know what unexpected expenses are coming your way, but we know they are coming (that sounds ominous doesn't it). This is why everybody needs a back-up plan or an emergency stash set aside to help when things go unexpectedly or urgently sideways. Because at some point you will need this and you don't want to be reaching for a credit card.

There's no doubt that these life events suck. But what can make them worse is when you can't afford them.

Amber: I remember as a kid my Dad worked for himself and we didn't get many holidays. One year he promised to take us to Sydney to the Royal Easter Show and I was super excited about it. Then we went to the beach one afternoon and Dad lost his keys at the beach. We searched everywhere but couldn't find them. They were gone. Keys to the house, keys to his car, garage keys, the whole lot. Gone. Dad had to call a locksmith and get all of his keys replaced. I have no idea how much that cost but it was enough that our holiday was cancelled.

Katherine: Not too long ago, my husband was finishing up the end of a contract and due to start a new role. Unfortunately, the role was cancelled a few days before it was supposed to start due to a key person passing away. He had to start looking for work all over again which ended up being seven weeks before securing and starting in a new role. The new job also paid monthly, so it was about 2.5 months without income. Fortunately, we had set aside an emergency fund, and as much as I hated dipping into those savings, I was certainly glad they were there.

These are the situations where it's tempting and seemingly easy to rely on your credit card. It may fix your immediate issue, but the expense still remains, leaving you in debt. Not all emergencies can be covered by a credit card, so it's much better to have a little something tucked away.

But how much should you have in your emergency fund? Well, a good rule of thumb is:
aim to have
three months' worth of household expenses set aside.

This means that if something very serious happens to you, you have a decent amount of time before money starts to get tight. This is not the same as three months' worth of wages. It's just your Everyday Expenses and Big Bills that we outlined in the budget chapter. If you were in a tough spot, you could always put your savings on hold and tighten your belt when it came to the non-essentials.

Let's say you are earning $60,000 per year. After tax, you would be banking just shy of $4,000 each month. Let's say your essentials make up 75% of this amount. This means that you need $3,000 and are capable of cutting back the remaining $1,000 in a pinch.

This means your emergency buffer goal would be $9,000.

Three times your living expenses is the goal everyone should be aiming for but we don't want you to get disheartened thinking that level of savings may be too difficult. Just remember that's the end goal. When you are first starting out, set your sights on building up an emergency fund of $1,000.

This account should be a priority before starting any of your Big Picture savings goals, Future Fun or additional debt repayments. If your savings capacity is small, it's time to get creative with selling things around the house you no longer need, working extra hours, or pulling in money via a side-hustle or the sharing economy until you have $1,000 in your emergency account.

Once you've got a minimum of $1,000, if you have high interest debts like credit cards, tackle those, but otherwise your next hurdle is to reach one months living expenses, then two months before hitting your final milestone of having three months living expenses set aside.

To help build up this account, continue to add to it when you can, whether it's through bonuses, tax refunds, or setting up an automatic transfer into your emergency fund account every week. It won't take long to add up. Even $20 a week will give you $1,040 over a year (and most people wouldn't really miss $20 from their paycheck each week).

This money needs to be out-of-sight, out-of-mind. Preferably a high interest bank account with a different provider than your everyday banking otherwise the temptation to spend it on non-genuine emergencies will always be there.

This isn't the account you dip into to buy Christmas presents or dining room chairs (this makes Amber sad... listen to our first podcast episode to find out why). It's for things that come up that are outside of your usual budgeting: insurance policy excess following a car accident or hospital stay, emergency plumbing call out fees and root canal. These are not happy things. These are the things that nobody wants to have happen to them.

Lastly, if you have three months worth of living expenses set aside. It gives you the option of having a longer waiting period on your income protection insurance cover. The difference in premiums between having a 30 day wait (which most people have) and a 90 day wait period is around 40%, so having an emergency fund will save you money on your insurance by allowing you to safely self-insure and increase your financial independence.

Once you have three-months-worth of living expenses, your confidence will soar knowing that whatever life throws your way, financially you'll be prepared. Having back-up, is what will allow you to get *back up* on your feet. So get your back-up plan started today.

CHAPTER 3

GET SUPER SORTED

$ $ $

So now that your Living Budget is sorted and chugging along. It's time to turbo charge your retirement. In this chapter, we will be talking about little changes that you can make now that will make a big impact. An early start now means avoiding drastic effort later on.

The great news is that some of these steps don't even require you to contribute extra to your superannuation account. Contributing extra to your super is something that you'll need to tackle at some point, but if you are strapped for cash, this chapter will include changes you can make that will boost your nest-egg without having any impact on your day-to-day cash flow. Cha-Ching!

We want to demystify superannuation, which is often massively misunderstood and get your retirement on track so your future self will thank you.

So what is superannuation?

Superannuation is not an investment in and of itself, it's an investment vehicle. It's actually a trust structure – and an extremely tax effective one at that. So when you hear people say, superannuation hasn't performed well that year, what they really should be saying is that the returns on the investments within their own super fund account wasn't great. Their returns may have sucked, but that may not be true for someone in the exact same super fund, but who has a different mix of investments within their account.

What if we put two investments in front of you? Investment A and Investment B. Both are great investments that are growing 6% each year. In fact you like your investment so much that you want to buy more. Under Investment A, you would earn money, lose some to tax then use the money you have left to buy more of that investment.

Under Investment B, instead of paying income tax first, you buy more of that investment and then what is left of your salary is what you pay income tax on. In short, Investment B means the cost to purchase that investment is less as you are doing it with your pre-tax income.

What if, I then told you that the income that your wonderful investment generated had to be taxed? (Isn't everything taxed these days?). In Investment A, for every dollar your investment pays to you in income, you lose about a third in tax (if you earn between $37,000 and $90,000 each year your income tax rate is 32.5%), but for Investment B, regardless of your income tax rate, you lose only around 15% - Less than half that amount!

Now, let's look at what happens when you sell your investments after retiring at age 60. For Investment A, if you aren't already feeling like you've paid your fair share of tax, you then have to pay capital gains tax and give a chunk of your profits back to the government as tax, but with Investment B, there was no capital gains tax and you get to keep the whole amount.

INVESTMENT A

INVESTMENT B

Well, these investments are identical. The only difference is Investment A is what happens when you purchase and own investments in your own name, and Investment B is the same investment, but owned through your super fund. At this point, super starts to look like a magical unicorn.

So what's the catch? Investing in your own name gives you a greater level of flexibility, but there is much more tax to pay along the way: from the money you earned which was taxed before you could even purchase the investment, tax on earnings the investment makes along the way and tax on the profit when you sell it.

Investing into your superannuation is certainly going to tick many boxes in terms of getting tax favoured treatment at multiple stages. The only drawback is that you can't access the money that you or your employer puts in until you meet a condition of release. For most people that is when you retire. There is also a limit to what you can contribute each year.

This is exactly what superannuation is. It is nothing more than an investment structure with a whole host of tax benefits attached that is designed to help set you up for a comfortable retirement.

So now that you know what superannuation is, it's time to start taking advantage of it. But wait you say. Do I really need to worry about all that? Can't I just access the age pension when I retire?

Here is a nerdy little fact: Superannuation only became compulsory in Australia in 1992 and the Australian Taxation Office reported that in its first year of existence, people with compulsory super accounts rose to cover 80% of employees. The rate at the time was 3%. It eventually increased to 9% in 2002-03. The current rate is 9.5% and there are plans to increase the level to 12%, but it's been a political football field and has been pushed back several years. As it stands, the increases to the contribution rate are set for the following dates. Note that this could change.

Superannuation Guarantee	
Date	**Contribution rate**
Current	9.50%
1-Jul-21	10%
1-Jul-22	10.50%
1-Jul-23	11%
1-Jul-24	11.50%
1-Jul-25	12%

Before super became compulsory, you would be very lucky indeed if you had an employer putting money into a pension account. For many people though, their only option was the age pension. When it first started in 1909, you had to wait until you were 65 years old before accessing the pension, but that was longer than most people's life expectancy at the time. If you were born in 1920, your life expectancy as a male was 59.2, and as a female was 63.3. When you stopped work, you had to be self-funded, and only if you lived longer than you were expected to, would you expect the government to help to look after you.

There are changes underway when it comes to the Age pension. The access age is gradually increasing from 65 to 67 and will be 67 for everyone by July 2023. So whilst the access age has been pushed back by 2 years, the life expectancy for Men and Women has increased by 20 years. That's a lot of time to spend in retirement on what was originally designed as an emergency income stream.

But as we spoke about in the introduction, who wants to spend 30 years living on the age pension when it's akin to living on the poverty line. *(The poverty line is considered to be 50% of median household disposable income. In Australia, the poverty line is defined as a single adult living on less than $433 a week and the old age pension is currently $466 a week)*

So unless that kind of lifestyle is particularly appealing to you, and if you are reading this book, we assume that you agree with us that the idea of aspiring to solely rely on the age pension sucks donkey-balls. So let's take full advantage of the opportunity that superannuation presents to get our money working hard for us so we can get the benefits both now and when we retire.

We now know that relying on the age pension is not a goal to aspire to and that superannuation is one of the most powerful tools we have that incentivises us to build our wealth, so where should we start when it comes to getting our super sorted?

Step 1

First things first. Don't throw your money away on unnecessary fees. This often happens when you have more than one account. If you have more than one superannuation account, odds are, you are throwing some of your money away. This is because many funds charge a monthly member or administration fee for each account that you have. Multiple accounts = multiple fees.

Because superannuation is a compulsory benefit for many employees, most employers will give you the option of using your current account, but if you don't provide them with details of your current fund, they will simply set up a new superannuation fund for you. Most people take the path of least resistance and simply allow their new employer to sort out their super for them.

How often do you meet people who have remained with the same employer their entire work life? These days it's uncommon to remain in the same job for 5 years let alone your entire work life.

This situation has left us with lots of people having more than one super account. In fact, as of 30 June 2018, over 15.6 million Australians had a super fund account (YAY!!!). But of these, almost 4 out of every 10 had more than one super account (BOO!!!!). That is over 5 million people who are potentially wasting away their superannuation!

So how do you make sure you are not one of them? Well the Australian Taxation Office (ATO) is here to help (oh my goodness – I never thought that sentence would come out of my mouth). Check out: https://www.ato.gov.au/forms/searching-for-lost-super/

The ATO is making it easier for you to find and consolidate any lost or unwanted superannuation accounts. On top of this, new legislation kicked off on 1 July 2019 designed to protect your superannuation entitlements. Superannuation providers are now required to send any accounts deemed as inactive low-balance accounts to the ATO. The

ATO will then work to reunite unclaimed super-money they hold for you into one of your active super accounts. Check out their website for more information. Make sure you are not one of the 5 million Australians who are potentially paying more fees than they have to and not taking full advantage of their super entitlements.

We have mixed feelings about this legislation. While it is designed to protect people from having their superannuation account balance eroded by unnecessary fees. The biggest issue is that the legislation carries risks of unintended consequences. For example, if you don't want these accounts to be consolidated, because you wish to keep the insurance cover attached to your super fund, you'll have to regularly engage with your super provider to ensure your account doesn't become deemed as "inactive". For most people this isn't something to worry about, but for those with health issues, or in risky occupations where it is difficult to get insurance cover, when these funds are consolidated, any insurance attached to these accounts is lost.

WARNING:

Before you close a superannuation account always check to see if there are any personal insurance benefits attached to your account. You need to make sure that you are able to get the levels and types of cover that you require before you close down any superannuation accounts. If you are in a high-risk occupation (eg police officer) or you have a health condition (eg diagnosed with chronic or ongoing condition like diabetes) this could prevent you from getting replacement personal insurance cover, or any future cover may have exclusions or medical loadings applied. So if you have insurance attached to your super fund and you close the account, you will lose this cover and may not be able to get it again. See our Get Secure Chapter for more info on personal insurance.

Step 2

Now that you know the first step is to avoid multiple superannuation accounts and where to go to find out how many accounts you already have, it's time to choose a superannuation fund. You probably have a few questions. Some of these might be.

- How do you know when you've got a "good" superannuation fund?
- What is reasonable in terms of the level of fees your superannuation fund charges?
- What investment options should you invest in?
- How much should you contribute?
- How much is "enough" super?

For such an important asset that will more than likely do most of the heavy lifting when it comes to your retirement, it's a bit strange that you probably didn't even choose your superannuation fund. It was probably opened for you by your employer. So given it wasn't a choice you made, how do you know whether they made a 'good' choice for you?

Some people judge their superannuation fund by its performance, other people by how low the fees are, while other people apply a completely different set of standards, such as whether their super fund allows them to invest in ethical options. Obviously good performance is important but looking at a fund and judging it purely by how it has performed in the past, is no way to guarantee that it will perform well into the future. Low fees are also important, but there is no point in having your money with a superannuation fund with the lowest fees if the returns are substandard. So what does a good superannuation fund look like?

Fees

Fees are an important consideration. Did you know that fees can have a massive impact on your account balance? For example, if your total annual fees are 2% of your account balance rather than 1%, the impact on your account balance after a period of 30 years will mean you will have roughly 20% less in your superannuation when you retire. Yikes!

When you're starting out, you want to focus on a low percentage-based fee. It's no good having a low account balance and being slugged with lots of admin fees. For example, if you've got an account balance of $5,000 and you're spending $300 or even $500 a year on fees, percentage wise, you're spending up to 10% on fees!!! That is outrageous! It may not be money that's coming out of your back pocket, but it is yours and it is real, and you better believe that it will have an impact on your future.

When you have a higher account balance, any small flat dollar based fees are usually less significant. If you've got a much higher account balance, the percentage based fees are what you need to pay most attention to.

Let's say you're sitting on $300,000 in your superannuation and you are paying 1% in fees, that's $3,000 a year on fees, if your fee is 2%, your fee has just doubled to $6,000!

There is no avoiding fees, so what's a fair fee to pay?

Our rule of thumb is that your total fees should be under 1% of your account balance and there are plenty, and we mean plenty of super funds with total fees below this level. Unfortunately, there are also plenty of super funds out there with fees of 2%-3% or even higher. We don't believe in the "Holy Grail" of super funds. It's a competitive market out there. And whatever fund had the lowest fees last year, probably won't be the fund with the lowest fees next year. If you are paying less than 0.8% in total fees, you're on a pretty sweet deal and you should high-five yourself immediately.

You should exclude any insurance premiums from your fee calculations because this is an optional expense that you can choose to include or exclude from your superannuation account. You should definitely assess whether this is a good deal, but this is a separate exercise we cover in our Chapter: Get Secure. You also need to exclude the government contribution tax. This is a tax of 15% that is paid on any contributions that your employer makes or where you haven't paid income tax such as salary-sacrifice contributions. This is not a fee charged from your superannuation fund. It is a government tax.

If your total fees are greater than 1%, we think it's time to look at alternate, lower-cost options, unless there is a particular benefit to staying, such as receiving matched contributions from your employer or some other service or benefit that you wouldn't want to lose such as your insurance.

So what kind of fees do super funds charge? Unfortunately there are several types of fees and charges when it comes to super, and some funds charge a single fee while others charge multiple layers. Most superannuation providers charge a combination of fixed-dollar-based fees along with percentage-based fees charged against the balance of your account.

We are going to help you understand the most common types of fees and then give you a simple script so you can call up your super fund to find out the type and level of fees you are paying each year.

The most common fees you'll come across are:

- **Member fee:** Usually a small flat dollar fee each month.

- **Admin fee:** Can also be a flat dollar fee each month, or a percentage fee based on your account balance. Some funds charge both a dollar fee and percentage.

- **Entry fee:** For every contribution you make, a percentage of your contributions is charged as a fee. This fee is far less common these days but accounts with these fees still exist.

- **Exit or withdrawal fee:** This fee is fortunately becoming less common. Usually a dollar-based fee is applied should you withdraw or roll-out your balance in part or full. Some older accounts have significant percentage based fees. So take care with this one.

- **Investment switching fee:** Usually this is a small dollar-based fee when you decide to change your investment option within the fund. Many funds offer a limited amount of fee-free switches each year.

- **Investment fees:** Sometimes called an "MER" and/or ICR, these fees are related to your specific investment option. e.g. "MySuper Balanced Option." This is a percentage-based fee. The fee varies based on the investment option selected. This fee is unlikely to show up in your account transactions. Instead, its impact is taken into account when determining the rates of return for your investment option.

- **Buy/sell spread fee** - You may pay this every time you make a transaction, including making a contribution, switching and

MAKE MONEY YOUR B!TCH

withdrawing. Typically, a small percentage fee on the amount being transacted.

- **Advice fees:** Can be either a one-off fee for personal advice provided about your account by either your super fund or a financial adviser. Like insurance premiums, this is an optional fee. This can also be charged as an ongoing percentage or dollar-based fee if you have a service agreement with an adviser. Any ongoing advice fees require you to agree with your adviser to renew/continue these service fees at least every 2 years.

We have some bad news, the fees listed above are not an exhaustive list. (We hear you groan and see you shaking your raised fist in frustration.) It's important to keep in mind that the most common fees that are likely to impact your account balance over the course of your working life, are the account admin fees and investment option fees.

Sometimes you may be in a low-fee superannuation account, but it is only the investment option fees that are making it uncompetitive. To lower your fees, it may be as simple as switching the investment option within your super account.

The lowest investment fee options are usually index-based funds because rather than trying to guess which shares will be the winners and losers, index funds invest in all or most of the stocks in an index. Indexes cover almost every industry sector and asset class, including Australian and International shares, property, bonds and cash. The investment manager isn't constantly trading, so the fees are lower. It also means that you get a wide spread of investments. This is called diversification, in other words, not putting all your eggs in one basket.

Personally we are fans of low-cost, index-based options. If it's good enough for one of the world's greatest investors Warren Buffet, it's good enough for us!

Okay, so I get that super funds can be a pain in the arse when it comes to understanding what fees I'm paying. How do I find out what fees apply to me? We are glad you asked.

You can find this information in a document called a Product Disclosure Statement which is also known in the industry as a PDS. This is a document that technically you are supposed to read, but most mere mortals will never read these documents. If you are one of the few who have read your super fund PDS you probably felt as though you were reading a document dedicated to worshipping the fine print filled with legal terms and industry jargon.

To make it seem easier, some providers split these up into multiple parts. Probably not the sequel you had planned to read in your downtime. So we don't blame you if you find it to be complicated or simply just another thing that you'd rather NOT be doing.

Don't worry, if the idea is as unappealing to you as it is for Amber (Katherine on the other hand loves to get professionally nerdy on the details), we're not going to make you read the PDS.

For a less painful way to find out how much fees you are currently paying we recommend calling up your current super fund and asking them the following questions. Make sure you have a pen and paper handy. This will help you understand the fees you pay, as well as learn some other handy info.

"Hi,

I'd like to know about the fees and features of my superannuation account.

Do I pay any fixed dollar or percentage based member or administration fees? What are they?
(note you may pay both a dollar and percentage based fee)

What Investment Option am I currently in and what's the underlying fee for that option?

What has the investment performance been for the last:
12 months?
3 years?
5 years?
10 years?
(note your investment option(s) may not have a long performance history or measure all these periods)

Are there any fees for changing my investment option?

Are there any fees for making contributions, or withdrawals such as partial roll-overs?

Are there any other fees on my account?

Can I make changes to my account online or have the option of sending in forms via email? *(Note: even if a fund accepts electronic forms, some actions such as a change of name, may require certified ID to be posted to the fund.)*

What is the break down of the asset classes within my investment option?

Are there any other benefits associated with having my superannuation account with you?

Thank you"

Well done. You have just uncovered how much you are paying in fees, and may have discovered benefits that you didn't even know you had access to.

If you happen to have multiple superannuation accounts, when you assess the fees, remember to consider your combined superannuation account balances as a percentage. An account balance of $10,000 paying $300 per year in fees may seem low but works out to be 3% in fees, whereas an account balance of $100,000 paying $1,500 in fees may seem significantly higher, is actually lower at 1.5%. So if you are considering consolidating multiple superannuation accounts, always base it on the combined balances of your accounts.

If the idea of even making a phone call still makes you want to run a mile, you can outsource this task to an adviser who will charge you a fee for their time. Your adviser can help with just the research, or provide a full service of recommending which account is well suited to your needs and assist you with consolidating your accounts and/or updating your account details.

Now that you are done with researching the fees on your account, we need to point out that fees aren't everything. There are other factors to consider, namely investment performance.

We love any super fund that offers a combination of low fees and above average returns.

Do your own research and make sure you look at both the investment returns and the fees. Just remember, that past performance isn't a guarantee of future performance. This year's top performing fund may not be next year's, but just like when you are facing excessive fees, if you have a super fund with consistently shite returns, it's time to look at an alternate investment mix or a new superannuation provider.

Fortunately, there are several websites that make it easy for you to compare the performance of many superannuation investment fund options. One of these is the super ratings website. It has a section that rates the top 10 performing super funds broken down by the asset classes or investment mix options you are interested in, based on different time-span periods. The longer the performance period, the better (well in our opinion anyway).

To save you the work, we've listed the Top 5 performing superfund investments for both Balanced and High Growth options as of 30th September 2019 according to the super ratings website. The top 10 list is reported each month, so to check out the most up-to-date rankings, head to their website at https://www.superratings.com.au/superratings-top-10/

It's important to make sure that when you are comparing the performance of any given investment option that you are making a "like for like" comparison. The returns for a "Balanced" fund will be different from the returns for a "Growth", "High Growth", "Moderate" or any other pre-mix option as they will each have different investment strategies.

Top 5 Performing BALANCED investment Options

Rank	Fund Investment Option	Return	Return Period
1	AustralianSuper - Balanced	9.55%	5 year
2	Hostplus - Balanced	9.50%	5 year
3	UniSuper Accum (1) - Balanced	9.39%	5 year
4	Cbus - Growth (Cbus MySuper)	9.09%	5 year
5	MTAA Super - My AutoSuper	9.06%	5 year

Top 5 Performing HIGH GROWTH investment Options

Rank	Fund Investment Option	Return	Return Period
1	UniSuper Accum (1) - High Growth	10.98%	5 year
2	Cbus - High Growth	10.28%	5 year
3	Equip MyFuture - Growth Plus	10.23%	5 year
4	MLC MKey - Horizon 6 - Share Portfolio	10.08%	5 year
5	NGS Super - Shares Plus	10.02%	5 year

You can always go straight to the website of your current super fund and check out their performance history. Many super funds will display the returns for each of their investment options for the following periods - 12 months, 3 years, 5 years, 10 years and so on.

Insider tip: Some super fund investment options are NOT true to label. It's big business to have the best performing "Balanced" option. Most people would think that a "Balanced" fund would "balance" their investment mix between defensive assets like cash, bonds and term deposits with growth assets such as shares and property. A sneaky trend in the industry to boost investment returns is to have sometimes less than 10% in defensive assets and +90% in higher-growth assets, but to still label the investment option as a "Balanced" option.

It's important to ask or look at the PDS for what assets make up your investment option to know whether it is true to label. If you aren't sure, call your super fund and ask for a break down of the asset classes within your investment option (see previous script).

Investment returns

So how do you know if the investment option in your super fund is performing well? How do you then choose what to invest your money in?

When it comes to super, if you were born after 1 July 1964, generally speaking you're not going to be able to touch your super until you have reached 60 years of age, and met a condition of release (retired for example). So if you are young, it could be a couple of decades or more before you can access your super.

When it comes to investing, you want to have your money invested where it earns you higher returns over the long term, but you still need to be able to sleep at night. Everybody has different levels of risk they are comfortable with and more often than not, it comes down to what stage of life you are in.

When you are young, you may feel more comfortable choosing a "high growth" or "aggressive" investment option that likely invests your funds mostly in shares both here in Australia and overseas along with other growth assets. This is because you have plenty of time to recover if the market crashes.

If you are closer to retirement, you might feel more inclined to choose an investment option that has less growth assets that produces lower returns, but also lowers the chances of you experiencing a negative return in any given year. But then again if you are closer to retirement and don't have enough funds, you may feel comfortable with remaining in higher growth funds and investments because you want to chase higher returns hoping the market will rally. It's all about what level of risk you are happy to live with over the time you have before retirement.

We're not going to lie about the future. How can we, it's not like we have a crystal ball. But we can tell you that if history is anything to go by, the odds are you are going to experience a market crash of some degree between now and retirement. In fact, you're probably going to experience several. So should you let that worry you when it comes to selecting your investment options?

Well, most people feel uncomfortable because it's not something they understand well.

The media loves to report on the share market and they make it seem like when it's going up, it's going to go up forever and when it's going down, it will spiral down into nothingness. But that's just not true. Yes there are both rallies (bull markets) and crashes (bear markets) and if you decide to sell a share for less than the price you paid for it, you can lose money. This is no different to any other item whether it's property or another asset.

Think of it this way, when is the best time to buy your favourite retail items whether it's a pair of shoes, a dress or the latest tech-gadget? When it is full price? Or when they announce a sale?

We love a retail bargain and we bet you do too. It's really no different when it comes to investing. Shares go on sale also. When the market is down and share prices are low, you can get more shares for your money. Every time you make a contribution to your superannuation you are investing. If the market is on a good run, you are probably happy that your investment is performing well. When the market dips, you may not be impressed that your superannuation or investment account balance is going down, but the money being contributed can purchase a lot more. As long as you don't sell, the loss is likely to only be temporary.

When Amber went on maternity leave, she had worked out how much money her family would need to cover the shortfall between her maternity leave wage and her family's living expenses while she was off work for 12 months. By the time she went on leave she had managed to save close to $20,000 in the bank. This money was to make up for the loss in Amber's wage and cover living expenses so that she could have 12 months off with her baby and the family would be ok financially.

Then the global financial crisis happened. Amber had not yet met Katherine, but she had watched the news most nights and was used to *seeing Commonwealth Bank (CBA) share price flit across the TV screen from time to time.*

She didn't own any shares herself but was curious about the stock market. One day she noticed that the price of a CBA shares were about $60 but not long after they had dropped to $28. Amber knew they were on sale and wanted to buy some and happened to have a lot of money in the bank. But she wasn't prepared to risk all of her maternity leave savings. What if $28 wasn't the bottom and she lost all of her savings and couldn't afford to take the time off work to spend with her baby? The risk was too great to invest everything and not one she was willing to pay. So she bought $500 worth of CBA shares (and had to figure out how to do that). Even though she felt nervous about the timing, she felt like she knew enough about the CBA to feel comfortable that it wasn't somehow going to go belly up. Later down the track Amber ended up selling her shares and more than doubled her money. Hooray.

In hindsight, her only regret now is that she could have invested her whole savings and maybe would be on a beach somewhere drinking G&Ts as we speak, but in her situation, at the time, that was too much of a risk. And that's fine. She has learnt to live with her decision (and only cries a little about it now). Risk versus reward is a very personal calculation and it has to be right for you and your family. These days Amber is prepared, knowing that for those who are ready, a market crash can be a once in a lifetime sale. When everyone else loses their heads, Amber is ready to pick up the bargain of a lifetime.

Picture this. House prices have had a great run over the last decade, making home ownership feel like a distant dream for many people. But if the house prices in your suburb dropped 10% and you are yet to purchase a home, or you've been planning to purchase an investment property, you may feel relieved that you can now finally afford to get into the market. If the market dropped by 20% or even 30% you may feel even more excited or relieved, but you may also feel worried that the market may drop further. Thing is you will never know until the moment has passed.

All investment carries some level of risk. There aren't many things that are certain in life and there will likely be several market crashes and accompanying market rallies throughout your lifetime. Yet history shows us that despite the ups and downs, over a long enough term, the market goes up.

So if you continue to have money go into your super fund or investments on a regular basis when the market is high, you will probably feel like everything is going great and you'll feel like you're getting great returns. But when the market crashes, and it will (and probably repeatedly, remind yourself that you are buying your investments or retirement savings when it's on sale. Buying shares is just like buying anything else, why would you purchase something at full price? We all love a bargain. So why not buy your investments on sale?

Super investments are also not all about shares. It's good to pick a fund that has some diversity. This can help spread the risk of poor returns by investing in a number of asset classes. In short, as the saying goes, "Don't put all of your eggs in one basket." When it comes to your super and other investments, this typically means investing in not only Australian shares, but in international shares and investing in other asset classes such as property, infrastructure, cash and bonds. What you are trying to do with a range of investments is have money in different areas so if a single sector or asset class performs poorly, you can average out your returns in other areas.

If this is starting to feel a little overwhelming, we have good news. Many super funds offer investment mixes that are pre-blended. Meaning they have done all the hard work for you. So a balanced fund is likely to have a mix of shares from both Australia and overseas along with investment into property and more secure investments such as government bonds. Most people have their superannuation accounts automatically invested into a pre-mix option. These often have names such as "Balanced", "Growth" or "Lifestage".

You may also want to have access to ethical or responsible investment options, and while access to investment options with this focus are on the rise, not all superannuation providers offer these options.

Growing your super

So you have a low-cost super fund, your super is consolidated and you are happy with your investment option – how much should you be contributing?

Well, that's not an easy question because it's linked to how much you want to have when you retire. In saying that, there are lots of studies that have been undertaken to work out how much money you might actually need. A notable one is the ASFA Retirement Standard.

https://www.superannuation.asn.au/resources/retirement-standard

This study says that for a comfortable lifestyle, an individual retiring in June 2019 would need about $43,600 per year in retirement whereas a couple will need $61,522 per year.

If you love your current lifestyle and you have completed your Living Budget, another way to determine your likely income needs in retirement is to make a copy of your Spending Plan then go through and delete all the expenses that you feel you will no longer need to include when you're retired. This could be mortgage repayments (working on the assumption you'll own your home outright by then), if you currently have children then removing any school or childcare fees, or other expenses such as income protection insurance or lower grocery bills and utilities if you plan to have a smaller home etc. Also add in things you might want to include in retirement (if you don't have them in your Living Budget already) perhaps yearly overseas holidays. This will give you an idea of your current lifestyle costs, that you can then aim for when you retire.

Long-range picture:
Long-range picture: How much will I need to maintain my current lifestyle in retirement? Start with making a copy

# of your Living Budget, delete the expenses that no longer apply and add in the ones that do!

Once you know your destination, it's then a matter of checking to see if you are on track to get there.

There are also plenty of calculators available online. ASIC's MoneySmart website (https://www.moneysmart.gov.au/) gives you access to a free retirement projector which will estimate how much you're likely to have based on how much you already have in super, how much you're contributing into super now, what rate of return you expect to receive and when you want to retire.

It will then estimate how much money you're likely to have in retirement and takes into account benefits that may supplement your super such as the age pension.

The projections are a useful guide, but they are only a guide as your actual returns are likely to vary, and it won't take into account significant changes in your income. However, it is a great place to begin to think and plan what you want for your future self.

No projection tool can give your exact figures, but they do give you a great starting point for planning ahead.

This is especially true for women. We are more likely to have gaps in our careers when we take time off for children. During this time when we are not generating income, contributions into our super will also cease. We are more likely to work part-time when we have young families which means we earn less money and our super contributions are less than our full-time peers.

A great rule of thumb to get started is to be contributing a minimum of 12% of your salary into superannuation. If you can manage 15%, even better. If you're like most Australians, your employer should be contributing 9.5% of your salary into super. As mentioned previously this number is scheduled to eventually increase towards 12% but this has been delayed a few times, so it could be delayed again. If your employer is contributing at 9.5%, you might want to top this up to 12% by contributing an additional 2.5% out of your salary or 5.5% if you want to get to 15%.

The sooner you start, the less you will have to do later on.

Let's say you began investing from age 20 for the first 10 years of your working life and then you never made another contribution ever again in your entire life, you would end up with more money than somebody who started investing at the age of 30 and continues to until the age of 60. Why is this?

It's all about time. Compound interest is very powerful so it's not about timing the market, it's about the time in the market.

https://www.moneysmart.gov.au/managing-your-money/saving/compound-interest

Case Study

Katherine is 20 (lol – that felt like a long time ago) and she has just started a new job. She has $100 per month spare which she can either spend or save. Katherine decides to save the full amount ($1,200 per year) in an investment that is going to return 7% per annum. Amber also started work but she decides to spend her $1,200 a year instead of saving it. (Her shoes were fabulous though!) But when she turns 30, she realises she might need to start saving. In the 11th year of this exercise, she starts to put away $1,200 per annum and she also manages to earn 7% on her investment.

Let's look at how much Amber and Katherine have each saved by the time they are 60.

	Year 1	Year 5	Year 10	Year 15	Year 20	Year 25	Year 30	Year 35	Year 40	TOTAL
Katherine	$1,200	$1,200	$1,200	$1,200	$1,200	$1,200	$1,200	$1,200	$1,200	$48,000
Earnings	$84	$483	$1,161	$2,111	$3,444	$5,313	$7,935	$11,612	$16,769	$208,331
End of Year Total	$1,284	$7,384	$17,740	$32,266	$52,638	$81,212	$121,288	$177,496	$256,331	$256,331
Amber	$0	$0	$0	$1,200	$1,200	$1,200	$1,200	$1,200	$1,200	$36,000
Earnings	$0	$0	$0	$483	$1,161	$2,111	$3,444	$5,313	$7,935	$85,288
End of Year Total	$0	$0	$0	$7,384	$17,740	$32,266	$52,638	$81,212	$121,288	$121,288

By starting to save 10 years earlier than Amber, Katherine has more than double the amount of savings by the time she is 60. Katherine only contributed $12,000 more over the 40 years, but it was the effect of compounding interest that more than doubled her earnings.

But what if Amber really knuckled down and instead of contributing $100 per month, she was able to start contributing $200 per month ($2,400 per year) to make up for lost time.

	Year 1	Year 5	Year 10	Year 15	Year 20	Year 25	Year 30	Year 35	Year 40	TOTAL
Amber	$0	$0	$0	$2,400	$2,400	$2,400	$2,400	$2,400	$2,400	$72,000
Earnings	$0	$0	$0	$966	$2,321	$4,222	$6,887	$10,626	$15,869	$170,575
End of Year Total	$0	$0	$0	$14,768	$35,481	$64,531	$105,276	$162,424	$242,575	$242,575

As you can see, Amber was able to just about catch up to Katherine, but she has to contribute 50% more of her own funds to end up with a similar balance at age 60. The lesson here, is that you can catch up, but the later you start, the more effort it will take on your part to get there (you may have to sacrifice more beautiful shoes on the altar of future financial security......)

The truth is that generally people are not very good at looking after their future self. YOLO (You Only Live Once) is not a new phenomenon. And Amber may be guilty of saying "that's future Amber's problem" (Amber: "I wish past Amber made better decisions!!!!! Damn her"). While it's true that starting early makes a big difference, it's also true that starting late is better than never starting at all.

So what if you are already past 30? Have you missed the boat? No!!! Get started now. The point is, the sooner you get onto this, the more money you will have when you retire. Because the more time your money has to compound, which is essentially when your money earns you more money, and then that money starts to earn more and more money and so the effect grows. The sooner you start the better.

> Katherine: *I once saw a young man coming to my office. He had finished university and entered the workforce at 22 years of age and on a decent income. He was lucky enough that his employer was paying just over 15% contributions into his super fund each year. His mum had always told him that he should contribute extra to super, so he did (what a good boy listening to his Mum!!!!)*
>
> *He decided to salary sacrifice $100 each fortnightly pay into his superannuation. By the time I saw him he'd been doing this for about six years. He had also invested into a high growth fund and by the age of 28 he had already accumulated $150,000 in his superannuation. This is more than most people have in their late 30s. When I asked him why he did it, he said, because his mum told him to. I told him that he owed his mum big-time and to keep on doing exactly what he was doing.*

The key is to set it up, automate it, so it never even reaches your bank account and the odds are you'll never even miss it.

Now if you feel as though your current financial situation is a little bit tight, you can start out small.

Start by asking your employer to salary sacrifice one percent of your salary. You will barely miss it. If you're earning $70,000 a year then we are talking about $700 of your salary over the course of the year. If you're getting paid weekly, this is about $15 into super and your take-home pay will reduce by about $10. I'm sure most of us can afford to give up $10 a week for something as important as our retirement.

When your pay increases or you find you have some capacity in your Living Budget, do it again and set aside another one percent until you work your way up to having 15 percent combined contributions.

An important note: You don't have to commit to this forever, but it is especially good if you can start before you have children. Once you have children, there is a lot more pressure on your household finances. You or your partner might decide to reduce the hours you work, you may have to pay for child care, there are also increased expenses such as food and clothing. If you need to cut back on any additional super contributions during this time to provide some cashflow relief, do it if you really need to, but if you can avoid it and continue to make those additional super contributions, even better.

Start before having children.

If you give your super a little bit of love and attention it will love you back tenfold in later years. So get into a good relationship with your superannuation and it will pay you dividends in the future - both figuratively and literally!

CHAPTER 4

GET SECURE

$ $ $

Let's face it, shit happens. Having a Living Budget that finally runs itself for the most part is great. Contributing extra into super and knowing your future is on track is also great. But what good is any of that if your income suddenly stops because your health takes a turn for the worse, or you accidentally get injured. The next thing you know, you're digging into all your savings or selling down the investments which may have taken you years to build up. If that isn't enough, are you then prepared to sell your home? If it comes to that, then what?

Like the parable about building on a good foundation, you need to make sure you are properly protected from the unexpected happening to you. We all like to think that bad things will never happen to us or our loved ones. But there are no guarantees. And the truth is, bad shit happens to good people every day. Being a good person doesn't give you immunity against cancer or car accidents. Being the most healthy person on the planet, may reduce your chances of lifestyle related diseases, but it won't stop an unlicensed and unregistered driver who is busy looking at their phone from running you off the road. In short, you need to get personal insurance to protect your biggest asset. You. Note, we are not talking about private health insurance. That's a different kettle of fish.

Odds are that if you own a property or a vehicle, that you probably have car and home and contents insurance. Why? Don't get us wrong, we think these covers are important. But think about why you have these covers. Is it because the idea of losing your car or home and having to start from scratch all over again seems like a setback that you just couldn't face? What are these assets worth? For a car it could be in the tens of thousands, and for most homes several hundred thousand dollars.

But what about your income? What's that worth? Well if you are 25 years old, you probably have 40 years worth of work in you. If you are earning $50,000 and never had a pay raise in your entire life, (which would completely suck). Over your 40 years, you would earn $2 million. If you were earning $100,000 it would be $4 million.

The truth is your biggest asset is your ability to work and make money. What's the point of having insurance to protect assets that are worth less, if you don't protect the one thing upon which all of that depends – your income. So let's make sure that your most valuable asset (you) is protected. Like all insurance, we hope you won't need it, but if you do, it will be worth its weight in gold!

The great news is that unlike your car and home insurances, some of your personal insurance covers can be funded from your superannuation, and some of them are tax deductible.

Not only that, the sooner you get your personal insurances sorted, the easier and cheaper it will be.

An important point to remember also, is that it's not only you that you are protecting, you are also protecting anyone that depends on you, whether it's your ability to earn money yourself, or the hours you put in caring for your family (or both). You are valuable in more ways than one!

There are many insurances that you will come across throughout your life. Most people insure their car, their home, and even their pets. But the last thing that they insure, is themselves. Ladies, it's time to get our priorities right, and make sure that all the efforts we are putting into leading our best lives both now and for the future can be realised – no matter what life throws at us.

The 4 Key Insurances

There are four personal insurances that you need to know about. They all come into play under different circumstances. So to make it easy for you, Katherine has shared the diagram that she draws for her clients to explain how they work together.

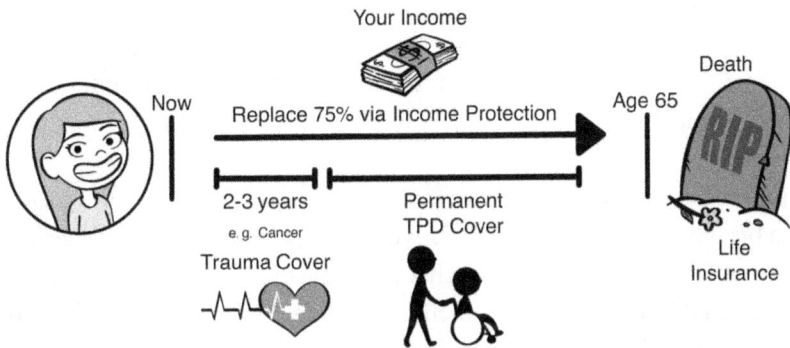

Above is a summary of what each cover does.

Life insurance can be sometimes called death insurance. It's insurance that will pay out if you die or doctors confirm that you have less than a year or two to live. Most people will use that insurance to:

- pay off their debts,
- cover funeral expenses,
- fund future education costs for any children,
- allow their partner to have some initial time off work following their death,
- allow their partner to make different work arrangements as needed to care for children;
- and lastly to replace any income that the family was depending upon.

If you are a young single person with no mortgage and no dependents, your needs for life cover are going to be very minimal. You may simply want enough to cover any small personal debts, your funeral, and if you were terminally ill, spending your final days on earth ticking off your bucket list items surrounded by the people important to you.

The second type of cover is **total and permanent disability (TPD)**. This is the cover that will provide you with massive financial aid in the form of a one-off lump sum payment if you find yourself in a situation where you can never ever work again. You can choose to be insured based on not being able to return to work in your "own" occupation, or "any" occupation.

Income protection insurance, typically replaces 75% of your wage if you become sick or get injured. This offers the broadest coverage because it covers you for medical events that impacts your ability to work to your full capacity. So what kind of things are you covered for? It is literally anything that impacts your physical or mental ability to work. You could be diagnosed with glandular fever, you could have cancer, you could need time off to recover from an elective surgery, you could have injured yourself playing sports or in a car accident. There are lots of different conditions that you can claim. Including mental health issues such as depression and anxiety.

One thing to note is that it is NOT job insurance. It is insuring your ability to work, not the availability of work. If you quit your job, get made redundant or fired, you are not covered. You also don't have to be completely off work, it can help cover the shortfall in your income if your health forces you to work less hours.

Now income protection insurance is different to most other insurance policies in that it has a waiting period before it pays out. Unlike car or home insurance which has a dollar based excess. This cover has a time-based excess which is called the waiting period. Most people have waiting periods of either 30 days or 90 days. If you can recover and return to work at your full capacity within that time, you probably won't receive any benefits. But if you are still off work after your waiting period has ended, the insurer will then replace 75% of your income.

You can generally remain on claim until one of two things happen. The first is that you can fully return to work or the second is that you reach the end of the benefit period, preferably your retirement age. Many super fund policies only have short benefit period such as 2 or 5 years. If that's the case, you better have a serious and credible back-up plan because if you are unable to generate income for the rest of your working life, you want to be covered right up to when you can get your hands on your super.

Lastly, income protection premiums are generally tax deductible, but this is because when you receive the benefits each month, you have to set aside money for income tax. In short, this cover allows you to continue to meet your financial commitments. Ideally, for most people, this should replace your income until age 65 when you would otherwise retire.

The final lump-sum cover is **trauma cover**. This is one of the insurances that people are most likely to claim. This cover has nothing to do with your ability to work as it pays out as a result of being diagnosed with one of the insured medical conditions. Most good policies cover 40 or 50 conditions. With full payment for more serious conditions and partial payments for less serious conditions such as low grade cancers or minor heart attacks etc. Despite the large list of conditions, about 90% of all claims come down to three areas being cancer, stroke and heart disease. If you are a young female, multiple sclerosis is also high on the list. Your chances of suffering one of the listed conditions is about 1 in 3, once you reach age 70, it's closer to 1 in 2.

So how much cover should I be considering?

Life insurance is the only insurance that is not about you. It's about everybody else that you leave behind. The other types of personal insurances: income, TPD and trauma benefit you while you are still alive to feel the impact and the other people in your life that depend on you. So if you do have a partner, talk about it with them in terms of what options they'd want if you died. Likewise, when they look at levels of cover, it's you that will feel the impact, so make sure you get a say in what outcomes you'll have if your partner dies.

Most people like to make sure that their debts die with them. But don't make the mistake of thinking that paying off your debts will be enough. Yes, paying off your debts is a great idea, BUT unless 100% of your income currently goes on debt repayments AND nothing else in your family's life will change, chances are you need to cover more than just your debts. You need to think about the shortfall and any other changes that may happen as a result of your (or your partner) not being around. You may have the ability to increase your hours at work, but if you have children, the last thing you want is to have your children lose one parent to death and the other remaining parent to work.

Both Amber and I have Life insurance, and plenty of it. It's the cheapest of all the insurances. If either of us or our partners died, we would both want to be:
- debt free,
- take 6 – 12 months off work,
- cover the gap in the income that's been lost,
- allow for any new expenses that may pop up such hiring an au pair or domestic help,
- we would also want the option of cutting back on the number of hours we work to be there for our kids,
- send our kids to our school of choice;

- or boost our retirement savings if we are suddenly facing only one retirement income.

In short neither of us wants to ever face the idea of having to consider a new relationship before we were ready simply because we needed a second income. We and our kids deserve better than that!

Knowing we will never find ourselves in this situation (financially at least) means that we no longer worry about the financial impacts. We even joke that if our husbands were to die, that it would all be very sad, but we would wipe our tears with hundred dollar bills at a very lavish funeral. So while we never hope to find ourselves in that situation, the peace of mind it provides, means one less worry in our lives.

TPD cover: My philosophy is that this cover should be partnered with Income Protection cover. If you could never work again, Income protection will replace 75% of your salary, but unless you can handle or enjoy the idea of a permanent 25% drop to your income, while probably facing new expenses, this cover is essential. If your rent or mortgage repayments take up 25% or more of your income, having a lump sum that wipes out your debts, or enables you to purchase a home outright, can offset the permanent drop in your income. However you likely have a debilitating illness or injury and that may mean you'll need a burst of money to modify your home and/or car to suit your new circumstances. You may face significant out-of-pocket medical expenses, and require ongoing care and support. The good news is that out of the four covers available, statistically, this is the one you are least likely to need, but if you do need it, it will make a massive difference to your situation because it only pays out when you are in the most dire situation.

Trauma insurance – like TPD cover, the odds are that you don't fancy a 25% drop in your income but unlike TPD cover, you're looking at covering a temporary situation. Cancer is the most common claim and it doesn't last forever. Being diagnosed with cancer is pretty scary and there would be a range of thoughts going through your head, none of them good. The last thing you want to do is be worried about money. One of three things can happen.

You'll either
   a) beat it and go back to a hundred percent of your former health and your work capacity,
   b) beat it, but the journey results in a permanent scar to your physical or mental health and your ability to work is permanently reduced or eliminated altogether or;
   c) you become terminally ill and pass away.

Under scenarios b and c you've got TPD and Life insurance to help with those outcomes. If you are one of the lucky ones and you recover fully (fingers crossed) you're all good, but what about the time it takes before you learn what your future holds.

That's where trauma insurance can help. Cancer and other serious illnesses also don't affect just one person. They affect your whole family. If you are being treated for a serious medical condition, then your partner or someone close to you, is going to be taking time off work to care for you during your treatment and, hopefully, recovery. If their income is reduced as well, you want protection.

But what if you have top of the line health cover? Australia is a great country to live in with great healthcare but that does not mean it is free. If you want a choice of doctor and to be treated faster, or to be able to afford treatments that are not on the PBS scheme (and there are lots), you will have some significant out-of-pocket medical expenses.

Trauma insurance is paid upon diagnosis. It means not relying on a Go Fund Me page literally gambling your life, and hoping on the kindness of strangers.

Income protection

As we've mentioned your income is your biggest asset. It's worth protecting. Income protection is typically designed to replace 75% of your income which includes your contributions to super. Most choices about this cover are around the features and optional extras.

Features where you must make a selection such as:

- how long should the waiting and benefit periods be,
- do you want basic or comprehensive definitions;
- and do you want any guarantees about how much you would be paid at claim time?

The options are extras that you can choose to include, or leave out entirely such as whether the insurer will increase your benefits while on claim.

Insider's Hot Tip: DO NOT, I repeat DO NOT rely solely on your superannuation income protection insurance policy!

When you fund **income protection insurance** wholly from your superannuation account, you have to meet a second hurdle to get your hands on the money which is the superannuation condition of release rules. The rules around super are constantly changing and there is a risk your cover or what you are entitled to can change and you might not have the protection you thought you had when you need to make a claim and it can leave you exposed. Furthermore, to be able to be funded from super, the policy is extremely basic and this is where people get into trouble with claims.

For example, one of these rules is that a superannuation fund can only release to you what you are earning at the time of the claim. But that means that if you are a mum currently on maternity leave and you're not earning anything and you suffer an injury, based on these rules, this money cannot be released to you. The premiums are cheaper, yes, but in my view, it's not worth the risk. Personal insurances found in super funds can definitely be part of an insurance strategy but you shouldn't rely on these alone if you are capable of getting better cover.

My point is most people don't actually expect their home to be utterly destroyed by fire. Though, it does happen from time to time, but the number one reason people lose their home (by a long shot) is because they lose the ability to service their mortgage because their income takes a hit or is completely lost after falling ill or suffering an injury.

We don't want you to have financial regrets or to become a statistic. Now you are equipped to do something about it, by protecting yourself, and those you love.

Case study

Let me tell you a story about catastrophe Carrie (name changed). Catastrophe Carrie came to see me in 2008. She was a mum with two young kids, earning a good income. Fortunately she took out a range of covers.

Two years later she went running in the Sydney City to Surf fun run. She woke up the next day and could barely move. She had suffered a bulging disc in her neck. She was unable to work for a couple of months. The insurer replaced her income.

A year or so later, having a routine pap smear test, Carrie found out she had a low-grade cervical cancer. She was able to make a claim on her trauma insurance policy. The insurer paid out 25% of her benefit (as it was a low-grade cancer) and life went back to normal.

A couple of years on (now a single mum) Carrie found herself getting tired and struggling with pain. Carrie was diagnosed with a form of arthritis that was causing problems and which was only going to get worse. Eventually Carrie had to leave her job because the treatment was not working. Her insurer replaced 75% of her income and will keep on doing so until she turns 65.

This wasn't the end of Carrie's story. A couple of years later Carrie developed breast cancer. The insurer paid out the rest of her Trauma insurance policy. Now that it has become clear that she won't ever be able to return to work, her TPD policy has been paid in full.

Carrie does not have her health back (although she did beat the cancer) and she would give anything to be back in good health. The good news is – she does not have to worry about money, while she continues to look after herself and her children. If she didn't have her covers in place, life would be a whole lot different.

Ok, ok, you've convinced me. But it all sounds very expensive. What's it going to cost me?

How much your cover will cost depends on a few factors.

Your level of cover will vary based on your needs and desired outcomes.

Your age – generally the younger you are the cheaper.

Your gender – Life cover is usually cheaper for women, but the reverse is true for Income cover.

Your occupation – A desk job carries much less risk than someone on the road all day for example.

Your smoking status – Duh!

Your BMI – If your BMI exceeds a certain level, you'll pay more. If it's ideal, you can get a discount.

Your premium structure – Do you want stepped or level premiums (explained later in this chapter)

Any relevant health factors – If you have a medical condition that puts you at higher risk of future health events, then it makes sense that you would have to pay more.

Options & Features - Most policies offer different levels of coverage from basic through to comprehensive as well as optional features and extras in addition to discounts for combining multiple covers.

So why is it cheaper and easier to get cover when I'm young? Think of it this way, your body is like driving a brand-new car out of the dealership that is perfect. There are no damages and it looks and smells great (I just had to throw that one in there). It is in perfect condition. Even with regular and scheduled servicing, cars don't stay in peak condition. They get older, pick up the odd rattle and eventually the engine wears out.

When we are young, most of us haven't had any major health events. Over time as we age and experience health events, cover gets harder to get. Your cover may be offered with an exclusion for past injuries or you need to pay extra because you represent a higher risk.

While all four of these covers can be paid from your personal cashflow, if you are strapped for cash, or prefer it, many people have the option of paying for their premiums via their super fund.

As mentioned above there are many factors which determine your premiums, but we want to be able to give you an estimate of what it may cost.

The estimates below are based on the scenario of a relatively healthy non-smoking female in an office-based role on "stepped" premiums. We've quoted the best deal we found as well as the worst to give you an idea of the range across different insurers.

Life insurance is cheap as chips and is one of the options that can usually be funded wholly from your superannuation account.

TPD: costs a little bit more than life insurance and can also be funded wholly from your superannuation account, but only if you are happy with the 'any' occupation definition. If you want the more premium 'own' definition, you'll have to at least pay for some of this out of your personal cash-flow.

Many people link their Life & TPD cover together. This reduces the cost of both policies.

For $500,000 of linked Life & TPD "Any Occupation" cover, the best and worst deals we found are outlined below.

Age	Lowest (per year)	Highest (per year)
25 year old	$348	$656
35 year old	$329	$966
45 year old	$648	$2,283
55 year old	$2,317	$6,453

The above premiums are based on your paying the cover personally. If you opted to have the premiums deducted from your super, your cover may be discounted by 15%.

Trauma insurance this is the only insurance that must be paid 100% from personal cash flow.

For $150,000 of top-of-the-line Trauma/Critical Illness cover, the best and worst deals we found are outlined below.

Age	Lowest (per month)	Highest (per month)
25 year old	$30	$62
35 year old	$39	$103
45 year old	$83	$193
55 year old	$186	$380

You may have noticed that as you age, cover gets more expensive. Very much so. These quotes were based on "Stepped" premiums. The only way to avoid age related increases each year is to use level premiums. So what's the difference?

Stepped premiums (age based) start out cheaper, but your premiums are re-rated every year in line with your age and generally the price goes up, even if your level of cover remains exactly the same.

The reason for this is as you get older, your health deteriorates, and the chance of something happening to you increases whether that's developing age-related conditions like arthritis, autoimmune problems, sporting injuries, or events like cancer or heart attacks that tend to happen in our later years. Now these can still happen to young people, but they are more prevalent as we get older. It's almost as if the cover is designed to become unaffordable at the moment we are most likely to need it.

If you only need cover for a short period of time this can be a good option. If you plan on holding this cover for a long time, it will likely end up costing you more than the alternative of level premiums.

Tip: Most covers that you receive automatically through your super fund are based on stepped premiums.

Level premiums (age locked) will start out higher than stepped premiums initially, but allows you to have your premiums charged at the rate for your age when the cover commences.

Just a heads up, it's not a "fixed" premium. Insurers regularly review their rates to match market conditions and to reflect what's been happening on the claims side across the board. This can result in the rate for your age either increasing or reducing, but you would still pay the rate that is applicable to the age you took out that cover. Over the life of a policy, you may pay only a quarter of what a stepped premium policy may cost but sometimes it is significantly less.

If you expect you'll need the cover for some time (such as paying off a mortgage etc) then this can save you a lot of money over the long term. The younger you are, usually the lower the rate will be and the more you'll save.

A level premium could be 50% more or even double the cost of a stepped premium initially, however some stepped premiums, can increase by a whopping 4,000% percent by the time you reach age 65.

We don't want to overwhelm you, but we do want to point out that there are a range of factors at play that you've probably never considered (and there are more we haven't listed).

We strongly suggest you get advice when it comes to personal insurance. It's something you cannot afford to get wrong. Having a base level of knowledge will help you better understand and assess any advice you receive.

Get advice

Sorting out your own personal insurance is like attempting to do your own electrical work. You may have a rough understanding of how it all works, but the moment you realised you got it wrong is the day that it's too late. The consequences may be irreversible.

There are lots of different options in terms of features and benefits and many of the words in the Product Disclosure Statements (PDS) have specific legal meaning and you will not know which ones are important and how much weight to give them. This is the job of a qualified financial adviser and preferably one who specialises in personal protection.

Insurance?
To get it right,
Get advice!

Insurance is something that is simply too important, so get it right, get advice. Many financial advisers will charge you only a small fee (or none at all) to research and recommend an appropriate insurance policy for you because they are likely to receive a commission from the insurance company. This is not an additional cost to you. If you took the quote from the adviser and went directly to the insurer, you will pay the same premium.

This is similar to when you use a mortgage broker to help find you the best home loan interest rate.

The role of your adviser is to help you work the levels of cover you may need or want. They will then find the best deal for you taking into account your health history and budget limits and can help you set it up the correct way. They can even negotiate with the insurer to get the best terms.

When it comes to claim time, having an adviser on your side, can also be useful. When you are in a hospital bed, the last thing you want to do is to complete paperwork. If you set up your policy through an adviser, they can deal with the insurer on your behalf to ensure that your claim is assessed quickly and fairly.

So not only will using an adviser save you a significant amount of time, you can leverage off their years of education, experience and insider knowledge, and all financial advisers have a legal duty to act in your best interests, giving you additional protection. In short, if you go it alone and get it wrong, you won't save any money (you may even pay more), and if you get it wrong, unfortunately you'll only have yourself to blame. Read the Get a Guru chapter which explains how to choose an adviser.

What about the policies I see advertised on TV?

Run. Run away! Unless of course you like the idea of going to purchase your favourite handbag only to find out it's a rip-off of the designer bag you actually wanted. Your new bag ends up falling apart days later spilling your personal contents in the most awkward situation and not only that, cost you double the price of the real deal.

It costs a lot of money to advertise on TV, so the markup is high on these policies. Not only that, they typically have lots of built-in exclusions which will mean you won't be able to claim on things like mental health conditions, pastimes such as contact sports, sometimes even one-off experiences like a single skydive. If a future health condition, can be traced back to signs and symptoms you had before the cover commenced (even if you had no idea) then the claim can be declined. In short, direct insurance can cost more and give you less.

A good policy guarantees to insure you based on the day you took out the cover, and it won't matter if you develop a chronic health condition, take up a crazy pastime, or develop bad habits. They are guaranteeing you insurance based on how your health was at the time you took out the policy and the terms of your policy can't be downgraded or even cancelled regardless of how many injuries or illnesses you experience.

Your Spending Plan and personal insurance make up the foundations of any future plans. Once you have both of these on track (and your retirement plans underway), you are safe to move on to designing and building the life you've always wanted.

CHAPTER 5

GET MORE MONEY

$ $ $

Who doesn't want more money? But how can we get more of it?

This chapter is not about asking the universe to recognise you as being worthy and magically waking up one day feeling like you can walk into your local hairdresser with a fat wad of $50 and start making it rain while singing Money-money-money, MONEY!

But hey, if that is your thing and it works for you, no judgement here and more power to you! Just let us know when you book your next hair appointment and we'll come along for the ride.

This is about **practical tips and ideas that you can do now to increase your earning power.**

One way is to ask for a pay raise. It's important to get pay raises. Every year the cost of living goes up and inflation affects everything you buy, from the cost of a loaf of bread, to transport and education. If your wage stays stagnant, you are actually falling behind. So even though it can be intimidating and scary, if you don't ask, you don't get, so let's get better at asking.

The skills and strategy you will learn in this chapter are transferable. You can use them whether you are delivering pizzas or working at a major corporation, regardless of the job. In every area of life, you will need the skills to have difficult conversations.

So we know it is important to ask for a pay raise, but how should you actually do it? An important step to take before you begin the conversation is to take the time to think and write down the value you bring to your role. What skills and experience do you bring to the job?

- Experience. Have you been in this job (or similar jobs) for a while? Are you more efficient and productive than when you first started or take less time than your peers to do the same role. Have you picked up additional skills?

- Education. Do you have qualifications that are relevant to your job? It doesn't have to be a degree but do you have a certificate in hospitality and are going for a job in a café?

- Do you mentor or train other staff? Do you increase the productivity of other staff members? Are you a good team player?

- Are you reliable?

Think about what you bring to the team and what your boss values in you. You need to be prepared for the conversation. But this conversation doesn't have to be hard or long or difficult.

Firstly, be confident. It can be as easy as a conversation with your boss that goes a little something like this.

You: *"I've been thinking about my role. It's been a little while since my wage was reviewed. Given I just finished my diploma/or my role now includes (insert task here), what are the chances of my pay going up $2000 a year?"*

If you are asking for a pay raise, we suggest you ask for between $2000 to $5000 more than you're already being paid, depending on how much you currently earn. This is not a whole lot of money spread over a year, so it won't sound like an outrageous request to your boss. But that's just a rule of thumb, and if you are on a six-figure income or have more experience, or there is a real cost benefit for your boss to give you a bigger pay raise, then we say go for it.

Women can sometimes pluck up the courage to ask for a pay raise but when it comes to talking about their reason for desiring a pay raise, they tend to talk about why they *need* the money. They say things like:

Can I please have a pay raise my rent has gone up and I can't afford it and I need more money.

This doesn't resonate with employers. Don't do this. The conversation should be about what you bring to the team and the value you bring. Not your own personal financial situation.

The number one reason people don't want to ask for a pay raise is a fear of rejection: What if your boss says no? And even worse than that, what if your boss says no and then is really angry at you for asking? This fear can be blown out of proportion. It's reasonable for you to ask for a pay raise, especially if you've given some thought to why you've become more valuable to the company now, or the job market in your industry has shifted.

It's unreasonable, but also unlikely for an employer to get upset about you starting a conversation. Just one word of warning though, make sure you don't make it an ultimatum. You are not saying, "Give me more money or I will leave."

You are saying, "Hey because of this reason, I think I'm worth more money to you." If they say 'no', that's fine. Just don't leave it there, follow it up with a question like, "When would you be open to a review? How does in six months sound?" If they agree, book it into your calendars, so the conversation doesn't get forgotten. We want you to go for it and not be too worried about your employer saying 'no'.

Using the 'if not now, then when' tactic is a great idea. If you've ever worked in a busy office, you probably know that asking to take annual leave with a bigger lead time increases your chances significantly of your request being approved. This is because a) you get in early before others, and b) it's something that doesn't impact them right now.

It's the same with a pay raise request, if you can't get it immediately, knowing it's been discussed before, by the time the review comes around, both you and your boss know you've agreed to a review. This creates a little more pressure on them to say 'yes'. It's not a guarantee, but it increases your chances by setting expectations for both of you.

I had an example recently of somebody who just needed a little more confidence. There was a new starter in my team, let's call her Leanne. I was talking to her about all of the on-boarding processes, including things like a start-date and it also included what level her wage should start at. Now I knew that her wage was a little higher than the one that we were offering as a standard base-rate starting salary, but I wanted her to ask for the pay raise. I wanted her to convince me that she was worth it. Our conversation went a little like this:

Me: *So are you happy to start on our base rate?*

Leanne: *Well the company that I'm coming from offers a little bit higher than the salary you're offering.*

Me: *Yes, I'm aware of that but are you happy to start on our base rate?*

She was quiet for a little for a moment and then she said: *Well when would I be eligible for a pay raise if I started at the base rate?*

Me: *Next year.*

I could see that she was getting uncomfortable and I knew that she wanted to start above the pay rate and I was actually willing to match her salary, but I needed her to ask for it.

Eventually, she said: *Given I have experience at this level and I'll be able to come in and manage a team straight away, would you please consider starting my pay above the base rate and have my salary matched.*

I said 'yes' and I was happy to do so. I just needed her to put the argument together to convince me. It was like she thought it was impolite to ask. It's not!!!!!! There's no hard feelings and I wasn't offended that she asked, but she was very timid and honestly, I almost counted it against her that she wasn't mature enough to have the conversation and to negotiate on her own behalf.

But what if that conversation had gone differently and I had said 'no'? What if you pluck up all of your courage and you get your thoughts together and you think you're worth more than what they're paying you right now. You then booked the time with your manager and you have the conversation and you're confident, and your manager says 'no'......?????? Well, I don't think that that's such a bad outcome anyway. You need to be proud of yourself for having the conversation and for pushing past your discomfort and asking anyway. But I also want you to remember that it's not only cash in your account that can be negotiated.

If your manager is unable to give you a pay raise because of business restraints or a tight fiscal environment a 'no' might be an understandable answer. But there are other things that you could ask for when a direct pay raise isn't on the table.

- **Paying for study:** You could ask for your work to pay for or subsidise some study, which is related to the job you are doing. If you want to go to university and you're working in a business and you want to study a business-related course or degree. It could be that your work is okay with paying for all or some of your course or university fees. I had some friends in university who did this; they had a contract with their employer that once they had completed university they would then go back and work for that employer for a number of years, maybe 3 to 5 years. But for them, they were happy to do it. The employer was helping them get through Uni and was guaranteeing themselves a workforce for a couple of years afterwards. Arrangements like these can be beneficial for both parties resulting in a win/win. But make sure you read the fine print. Some of these arrangements require you to pass subjects and if you fail, you are required to pay the money back to the company. So take it seriously and study hard.

- **Time off to study:** If your employer is not in a position to help you with your university costs, CIT or any kind of study fees, they might be willing to give you some paid time off to support you in your study. Study leave can be negotiated in some organisations and it can be used for maybe taking half a day off on Wednesdays, for example and leaving work to go home and study or going to lectures etc. whilst still being paid for that time.

- **Flexible working arrangements:** Instead of a pay raise, you could ask for some flexibility in your hours. While most people initially think of a request to work part-time, there are other types of flexible work arrangements. There are some people that I work with who work a nine day fortnight as part of their full time job. In short they have slightly longer work days for nine days a fortnight, something like 7:30 AM until 5:30 PM and then one day a fortnight they have off. They are compressing full time hours into 9 days, rather than 10 days each fortnight. This is no extra money in your account, but it means that you might use that extra time to study a course not related to your current job, spend time on a side hustle, reduce your child care fees or simply get some work-life balance and have a long weekend, every other weekend.

- **Work from home:** This of course will depend on the nature of your work. With many people working in office-style jobs and improvements in technology, working from home has become more accessible and acceptable than ever before. If you live in a city like Sydney, this could save you both time and money by not spending money on parking fees, fuel or your time on a lengthy commute. I (Amber) work from home one day every fortnight. For me, it means that I get to take my kids to school and when I return home I have some peace and quiet to clear a whole lot of documentation. This also minimises my distractions throughout the day as I am guaranteed a quiet place to work with minimal interruptions. I appreciate the flexibility and my employer still gets a full day's work out of me.

- **Extra super:** In Australia, employers must put a percentage of your wage into your nominated superannuation account (we have a whole chapter on this, so check that out if you need help choosing an account). But an alternate option to a pay raise to your wage that goes directly into your bank account is to ask for an increase in the rate of superannuation that is paid as part of your overall package. Given the power of compound interest, even 1% or 2% additional money into your super account over the years could add up to a whole lot of money when you retire.

- **More recreational leave.** It's standard in Australia in full time, ongoing employment for people to be eligible for 4 weeks rec leave a year. Some industries receive more leave than this such as police officers and teachers. If you can't increase your base pay, consider negotiating an extra week annual leave each year. Again, it's not extra money in your bank account, but it means that you have more time and resources to do the things that you value whether it's travelling or taking holidays, having the odd paid day here and there to recharge your batteries, or if you have children, being able to take more time off during the school holidays rather than having to pay for expensive school holiday programs or take leave without pay.

These are all options that you can consider before you go and have a conversation with your boss or your manager around a pay raise. Even better if you can negotiate items such as extra leave into your contract from your first day of employment.

Given this is a sensitive and difficult topic for people, I suggest you practice the conversation. It seems very strange I know, but get a friend or even an executive coach and practise selling yourself to them. Talk to them about why you are worth a pay raise or higher salary, what you're after and then get them to say 'no' to you. Yep, you heard that right, get them to say 'no'. That way you can practice steering the conversation to talk about some other options that you might like in lieu of a pay raise. The things that we've just covered such as flexible working arrangements, extra leave, extra super or working from home. Do it a couple of times to make sure that you feel more confident walking into the conversation.

Let them give you some feedback as well. Did you look down too much? Were your hands fidgeting or did you not know where to put your hands? All of these things can be really helpful to practice and can improve your negotiation techniques so when you're in the conversation, you can be focused on what you want.

When it comes to the real deal and you're talking with your employer, you'll feel more relaxed. Depending on the outcome, you may be over the moon if it goes well and have a graceful exit planned with a commitment to a future review, that will boost your chances in the future.

Some people think that they've missed the opportunity to have the discussion about a pay raise. You might think this discussion is only available to you when you start a new job and when you are negotiating your starting salary. But this isn't true. In fact, it can be easier to have a conversation if you're already in the workplace. Once you've started to deliver in the workplace and your boss can see the value that you bring to the team, and you've built some rapport, it can be even easier to have the conversation.

When you start in a team you are selling the potential or the promise, of what you will bring. But once you have been on the team for a little while, it's not potential anymore but realised deliverables. So, you haven't missed out. Even if you haven't had the conversation yet, it's not too late. Timing is important. Most companies have mid-year or end-of-year performance reviews and this is the perfect time to put your case forward.

So what about this: you've taken a job and you're under a collective agreement or an enterprise agreement? Which means you don't get to negotiate your pay-rate. Instead you're categorised and you're given a rate of pay. Even within these quite formal pay structures there is a range. You might start at the bottom of the range and you could be on something like $54,000 a year. The top of the range could be something like $62,000. So even in set formal pay structures, there is likely still the ability to negotiate. Instead of starting on the base salary perhaps you could negotiate starting one increment up, so maybe starting at $56,000.

Any extra money that you are able to negotiate is not just extra money in your salary every payday. It also means extra money into your super. A higher wage means your employer's contribution into your super account is higher. It also means you have more money available to pay off debt faster (check out our "Get the Heck Out" chapter for strategies on how to do this) or you could invest more money (check out our "Get Rich" chapter for how to invest).

Now $2,000 extra a year might not seem like a lot of money every week (it's $38 before tax), but it adds up. So be brave and ask!

CHAPTER 6

GET RICH

— $ $ $ —

So who doesn't want more money to do the things that they want to do? Being rich means different things to different people. For some it's about being able to drive the car of their dreams. For others it's about being able to take an overseas holiday every year. For others it's about having a certain amount of dollars in the bank. Whatever it is to you, get clear about it and then you can start to work towards your goal.

Getting rich usually takes planning and time, unless you're one of those lucky few who have a sizable inheritance coming their way or you manage to become a lottery winner (and if you did, please buy us a ticket too!!!). For most of us, we need to create good habits. Which is what this chapter is about, to teach you to create habits now that will get you where you want to be, because **getting rich is a habit, not a one-off event.**

The most important thing is, just to get started and do something. Sometimes people get caught up on finding the unicorn, THE best investment or they are waiting for THE perfect or THE best solution,

when at the end of the day, the biggest difference you can make is just simply start.

In this chapter we will talk you through the different forms of investing and perhaps you may find one that you feel more comfortable with than others. Either way, these will all help you form good habits and can help get you where you want to go.

Important note. In some sections we mention some product providers by name. That doesn't mean it's a personal recommendation, because at the end of the day we know nothing about your personal situation. It's purely for information purposes and you need to do your own research to decide if any products or investment ideas discussed are suitable for you. Better yet, get personal tailored advice from a suitably qualified professional.

So let's get started. Now that we've already completed the Living Budget chapter from earlier in the book, we are now going to use that spare income that you've identified to make a difference in your life.

Spare change investing

What is spare change investing? It's also called micro-investing and it works on the basis of setting aside and investing small amounts. It's unlikely that you will miss those bits of change and over time, rather than fritter 50 cents away here and there, you could instead end up with a nice little nest egg.

Some of the most popular products out there right now to help people invest small amounts of money is *Raiz (formerly known as Acorns) and Spaceship Voyager. It's a matter of downloading the app on your phone and linking the app to your chosen bank account. Though both of these micro investment apps have slightly different offerings.*

Raiz

Raiz has a nifty feature called "round-ups" that help you invest automatically. You link Raiz with your bank account and it tracks your spending. It works like this: every time you spend money from your bank account, the transaction gets rounded up (usually to the nearest dollar) and this amount gets invested. For example, you could buy a coffee for $3.50. This would then be rounded up to the nearest dollar, e.g. $4. Once these 'round-ups' reach $5 it will then get invested in a diversified portfolio of shares and bonds from around the world. And you can choose 1 of 6 different portfolios based on how aggressive or conservative you want your investment to be.

If you want to invest a little more than your spare change, you can make additional one-off or regular direct debit contributions whether it is daily, weekly, fortnightly or monthly into your account.

This system works best when you combine both the rounding up and regular contributions feature. With the obvious reason being that the more you put in, the faster it grows. You can start with something as little as $5 per contribution along with your Roundup transactions. This money will be set aside and build up in an account that is separate from your everyday banking.

You may even receive referral bonuses. Raiz tends to give $5 to both you and your friend if they sign up using your referral code. From time-to-time they run promotions where the referral amount is doubled to $10 each.

In terms of fees, Raiz charges $2.50 per month if your account balance is under $10k. After that, it's percentage based instead of the monthly fee.

Spaceship Voyager

Spaceship came onto the scene in early 2018 and offers just 2 investment options. Spaceship Voyager has built a portfolio of companies that they believe represent the future. Companies like Tesla, Apple, Netflix, Amazon etc. If you prefer something with a bit more of a traditional mix then you can also invest in their 'index' portfolio. It's basically just an index fund made up of the top 200 companies.

You can set up regular recurring investments on Spaceship. However, there is no round up feature.

Voyager has offered more generous referral signup bonuses of $20 in the past, but this seems to be pretty rare.

The good news is that the first $5k invested in Spaceship is fee free. After that, it's just a small percentage fee.

Both of us have tested out the Raiz app and over the last two years from the roundups and the weekly deduction of $10 Amber has managed to save $1,300 in her Raiz account. Katherine has had hers for a little longer and recently hit $2k in her account. Both of us feel that if we hadn't been using the app squirrelling away small amounts, that money would have been spent on things that neither of us would even remember. But instead it's become a meaningful amount which can be used to do something that we will absolutely remember and cherish.

What if you like the round-up feature, but don't want to invest?

Several banks now offer this feature including ING, UP and Bank Australia. We're sure there are probably more as it's becoming increasingly popular. It works on the same premise, except that instead of being invested, the money is swept into a linked savings account. A handy feature is that the money is usually swept away at the same time as the transaction, rather than waiting until it has built up to a minimum level. Both UP and ING will even allow you to round up to the nearest $5.(check out our Money Maddams podcast episode 6, where we interviewed UP bank representatives to find out more about their product features)

Banks like UP even offers the $5 bonus sign up feature for each friend you refer and signs up.

So what about other investments like shares and property?

Shares in their simplest form are simply owning part of a company. This could be your own business or a major corporation listed on the stock exchange like BHP, NRMA, CBA, Coca-Cola or Apple. For the purpose of this section we are talking about the latter, shares that you can buy and sell on an open market.

Shares can provide investment returns in two ways. Income in the form of dividends (which is the company giving you a share of their declared profits) or the value of your share may increase allowing you to sell at a profit, but it may also fall.

There are a myriad of shares out there to choose from, both in Australia and overseas.

When it comes to choosing shares, my personal belief is – go with what you know and understand. This may for example be a company where you already use their products and services. Such as the bank or credit union where you hold your home loan, your electricity company, car insurer, technology provider, or grocery store. You get the idea. If you contribute to their profits by being their customer, why not share in those profits?

Now for some, shares are scary because the value of their shares can increase or fall. But this can be an advantage. Just like the Boxing Day or Black Friday sales, it's great to buy shares when they go on sale which allows you to purchase more of them for less. When they are performing well, then chances are you are feeling pretty chuffed and if you were to sell them, you could make a nifty profit.

Another advantage with shares is the dividend payment. The income that shares produce is called a dividend and it can either be paid directly to you or be automatically reinvested to purchase more shares (which can help in building up your investments and it can be done on autopilot, making it super easy for you).

Australian shares can also come with what's called a franking credit. This means that the company has already paid tax on their profits before giving you your share of the dividend. If you are a high income earner, you'll only have to pay tax on the difference, if you are a lower income earner there may be no additional tax to pay, or you may receive a tax refund at the end of the year.

In short, shares can provide a very tax-effective form of income.

You don't need thousands of dollars to start investing in shares, but you will typically pay a fee of $20 to $30 each time you buy and sell shares. So unlike micro investing, you may want to avoid investing frequent smaller amounts.

Shares are also relatively easy to buy and sell. Our view is that shares and property should be viewed as long term investments. If you find yourself needing access to funds, you can sell a portion of your share holdings, and don't have to sell the whole lot. This is entirely different to an investment property as you can't sell just the kitchen if you need the cash.

Now most Australians love the idea of investing in property. It's the great Australian dream and we have been sold the idea that you can't lose money from houses (It's 'safe as houses', right?) Property feels safe.

It's easy to understand because you can see it. It has a physical aspect to it; you know what you're buying. But for me, I actually view this as a riskier and more expensive option and I'll tell you why.

If you purchase one property, it is simply one property. All the risk is held in that one location. When it comes to shares you can access a wide range, across different industries and different sectors, in different countries, to help smooth out any variation on returns and diversify the risk. In short, with shares, it's easier to spread the risk than with property, where you may have all your eggs in one basket.

Property is the only investment to get taxed at all three stages of ownership. You pay stamp duty when you purchase, (which can be significant), land tax while it is rented out, and capital gains tax when it is sold.

Property is also a much bigger purchase commitment and usually means taking on debt. Now investment debt is not a bad thing. Because it's linked to an asset that should grow and the interest in many cases can be tax deductible, but it does increase the risks you face.

If you purchased a property for $500,000 and let's say you borrowed $400,000. There are not just the repayments that you need to consider. Interest rates are at historic lows at the moment, but they can and will change. The entry and exit costs for purchasing and selling property can be high. There is stamp duty, insurances, rates, body corporate fees, water usage charges, property maintenance, conveyancing and legal fees and usually an agent selling fee. This makes getting in and out of a property expensive and can take a lengthy time. There is also worry around tenants, property damage and vacancy rates to consider.

Now what if you invested into a portfolio of shares, what costs would you face? For starters you can start with a much lower commitment, but let's assume you've invested the same amount in the above scenario and you also borrowed the same amount. You wouldn't pay any entry fee or exit fees beyond the brokerage fees. There are no ongoing rate notices, repair costs, utility or insurance bills to pay or pesky tenants to deal with.

Though you would still be subject to interest rate movements, and instead of receiving rental income each month, you'd receive dividend payments which wouldn't be a set amount each month. For us, this makes shares much less complicated.

The worry most people associate with shares is around the short-term fluctuation in value or they don't feel they understand the idea of shares well enough to feel confident in their decision. However, if you view shares as something you would hold long-term like most people do for property, the variations in value smooth out over time and historically have been a great performer.

Just to be clear, we are not anti-investment property, one of us is the daughter of a real estate agent who was and is a big believer in the power of investing in property. We simply feel it's important to highlight the differences for each when it comes to the likely costs, complications and the level of ease or difficulty involved.

Regardless of your preference, both of these options need to be viewed as a long-term strategy.

What about a high interest savings account and term deposits?

Given current interest rates, we think of these as holding accounts rather than investments. The rate of return that you are going to get at the moment is really low. Right now, you would be lucky to get more than 2% to 3% and you then have to pay income tax on any interest earned. The average punter will lose about a third of the interest to tax. This means that your money is barely keeping pace with inflation.

Term deposits are much less popular these days, because they don't tend to offer much more than most high interest savings accounts, and there are usually penalties if you want to access your money before the term is up. However, this can be a good incentive not to touch your money if temptation is a problem for you.

These products are tools that you can use to help you in the short-term but they are not a good long-term solution to increase your wealth. It is significantly harder and will take a lot, lot longer to build and grow wealth via cash and term deposits only.

What about managed funds?

Managed funds are what make up the investments in most superannuation accounts. Managed funds are simply parcels of investments where an investment manager, pools your money with other investors and invests your money for you. Each managed fund will have its own theme or purpose. Some managed funds include a wide mix and spread of different assets, whereas others can have a niche focus such as in investing in tech-based companies, or commercial and retail properties or government and corporate bonds. Others specialize in investing in overseas markets, like the US or Japanese markets, or some may focus solely on Australian shares, etc.

In short, you can easily spread your money and invest in opportunities and in companies you may not normally be able to access on your own.

Index-style managed funds are usually the lowest cost options as there is very little trading costs involved. They simply aim to capture the returns of a given market such as the top 200 companies on the Australian Share market for example.

Other investment managers try to predict the winners and losers, they may perform better, or worse, but it means their fees are higher. More often than not, the increased fee outweighs any improvement in the returns they generate.

What about investment bonds?

An investment bond is similar to superannuation in that it is not an investment itself, it's a structure with its own set of rules and tax benefits.

Like super, the money you invest is typically invested into a portfolio of managed funds. The provider lets you choose, so if you like to invest in a mix of Australian shares and property securities, you can do that.

Unlike super, you can access your money in the bond at any time. However, there are still tax incentives. Like super, there is no personal tax liability while your money is invested, it is all taxed internally and there is nothing for you to declare on your income tax return. If you leave your money invested for 10 years or more, when you eventually access those funds, there are no capital gains tax payable. This can save you a lot of money, because at the end of the day it's the money you get to keep that counts.

So Investment bonds can work really well as a long-term strategy. Offering both tax incentives while retaining flexibility to access the funds if needed.

Investment bonds can start with a small amount such as $1,000 and offer the option of setting up a regular savings plan. These usually require at least $100 each month.

Regular investment plans can help with creating new habits. If you treat your investments like a bill that you pay every month, it will build up without you even realising.

Investment Bonds can be very useful for funding longer-term goals. Let's look at this case study: a couple came to see me, let's call them Bob and Jane. They came to me because they love their lifestyle and have jobs that pay well but they can't see themselves working until 60 or 65. They want to make sure they can stop work, if they want to, at age 50 and still have an income to live on before they can get their hands on their super (at age 60). They are looking at being able to self-fund an early retirement. To cover this gap, I recommended they set up an investment bond. They contribute to it each month with a plan that one day when they stop work, they will access these funds which will provide a pension and this will replace their regular wages between the time they stop work and when their super becomes available.

Another way you could use an investment bond, is to help pay off your mortgage. Let's say you've tried your best at making extra repayments and paying off your home loan faster but the temptation just gets the better of you and you keep on drawing on your offset or redraw account.

Some people prefer investment bonds because it's out of sight, out of mind. Or because they have a fixed loan rate which limits their ability to make extra loan repayments. So instead, they direct spare cash flow into an investment bond. After 10 years, they don't have to pay capital gains tax and they take the money out of the bond and use it as a lump sum payment on their mortgage. This works best when self-control is a serious problem, or what you can earn from investing is better than the interest savings on your mortgage.

Investment Bonds are also a popular choice for setting aside money for future education costs. If you have children, you'll probably have been approached in a shopping mall at some stage by groups that promote the ability to help you set aside funds for higher education costs. The notion is great, but usually it's a poor to average outcome and you'd probably be better off just putting the money in the bank. Particularly if your child wishes to pursue a career that doesn't involve university, then those products won't net you any real benefits.

With an investment bond, you have the ability to set aside the money where it has the potential to earn a higher rate of return. Whether you have a goal helping your child get into their first home, or to pay for university, it's about whatever is important to you. The point is that no one is going to dictate to you what you have to use it for, so you get better flexibility and control.

So what about just parking the money into a bank account in your kid's name? Well there are a couple of issues here: the first is that if you use an everyday banking account, you can probably see it in your online banking balance and it's going to be a temptation, despite your best intentions. Secondly, there's only so much money and interest that a kid can earn before they too have to start paying tax. Plus, the government actively discourages people from putting large sums of money in their children's name. Children pay penalty tax on their investment earnings which can be as high as 66%! That is right – 66%. This is to stop parents from trying to hide money in their kids' names and believe me, it is a good deterrent to stop people from doing that. If you have a generous family member and have been disciplined in saving their birthday or pocket monies, then a bank account in the child's name will work against them.

An investment bond doesn't have that problem because it is taxed internally – currently 30% (even less after franking credits) and you don't need a tax file number. Unlike a bank account, the money is going to be invested in assets which have the opportunity to grow and you can choose an investment option within the bond that suits your comfort level. If you've got a long-term mindset, which is what these investment bonds are all about, you should get a much better rate of return when compared to sitting in a cash account for the same period.

This all sounds great on paper but when it's my hard-earned money, I don't want to lose any of it.

Let's talk about attitudes and headspace. When it comes to investing, there's no such thing as a risk-free option. Most people are pretty comfortable with property but get scared when it comes to investing in things like shares and managed funds because the value can go up and down. (Property values can go up and down too, but there seems to be a higher level of comfort about those numbers.) If you don't commit part of your money to investing (in whatever option you choose) there is a very real risk that you will experience a different kind of loss. You may fail to grow your investments to the level you need for a comfortable, fulfilling retirement.

In other words, playing it safe, may mean missed opportunities to grow your money.

There are a couple of different ways you can tackle some of this, different ways to think about it. The first is education. Make sure you feel comfortable with your level of understanding. Sometimes the best way to do this is to wet your feet, with a small amount until you feel more comfortable and familiar.

Perhaps you are worried about when you should start investing as you are worried that the market could drop dramatically once your money is invested. One way to manage this is with a strategy known as dollar cost averaging which can reduce any timing risk. Let's say you have $10,000 to invest. You could invest it all in one go, or you could drip feed your money through a series of regular and smaller contributions into your investments. However, whilst you are reducing this risk, you may also risk reducing your rate of return if the markets go up as you invest.

If you have superannuation, you are already an investor, and it's almost a certainty that at some point, you're going to experience a market crash. It may help you to stick to your investment strategy if you think about a market crash like you would for Boxing day or Black Friday sales.

I think about my investments the same way I do for shoes. I hate paying full price. I would always rather buy them on sale. Who wouldn't, right? Why? Because you save money and get a good product at a lower price. Well, it's the exact same with investing. When your investments are performing, it's great and you get to see the benefits. When your investments are down, your money can go further by allowing you to buy more of the same thing at a lower price.

Let's look at the global financial crisis as an example. Prior to the crash, everybody was loving the stock market returns. It was beautiful returns of 10, 11, 12% or more per year. When it crashed over a period of 18 months, it lost close to 50% of the value. Now this market is made up of a lot of household company names like CBA, BHP, Apple etc. These are big companies that weren't going anywhere and yet their stock prices plummeted. They were on sale!!!!

You also only lose money on shares if you choose to sell them while they are down. Some years back, I had been watching the share price of Xero (an accounting software company). I liked their software and I knew that their share price had steadily increased from $4 to $40. I was certainly wishing I had got in on that one in the early days. One day I saw their share prices plummet from around about $40 to $30. At this point I decided to buy some shares (woohoo 25% off), but this wasn't the bottom and they dropped further, so I purchased some more at $25 and then some more again at $17. Eventually they hit a low of around $12. I felt like I got a great deal, but I must admit that by the time they got to $12, I was starting to feel a bit worried but the share price eventually bounced back. And I sold the shares after they beat the previous high of $40. Today Xero shares are sitting at $68.

In short, prices go up and down. When they're down you get to buy more of them, they are better value for money. When prices go up again, you own more of those shares. Investing regularly will help you average out the peaks and troughs. Over the long-term, typically shares go up but don't be afraid of a pullback in the market. it's usually temporary (especially if it's not just a single company). Over the long-term, it should pull through and go on to reach new heights.

As one of the world's most successful investors, Warren Buffett puts it, "If you aren't willing to own a stock for 10 years, don't even think about owning it for 10 minutes."

No investment is without risk therefore you should never invest more than you feel comfortable with. If it's causing you to lose sleep at night, then it's probably not the right investment for you. Your confidence is likely to grow with experience, so make a start even if it's small so you can invest in your education. Sometimes experience is the best education.

So whether you plan to build your wealth through micro-investing, managed funds, shares or purchasing an investment property or decide to use structures like superannuation or an investment bond, the key is simple. Avoid getting caught up in selecting THE best single solution. If you do that, you may never start. Whatever path you take, do your research, consider your timeline, and seek professional advice before making any major decisions.

CHAPTER 7

GET YOUR PAD

— $ $ $ —

There is no doubt that owning your own home is part of the classic Australian dream. Though for some, renting will be their best option. If you aspire to purchase your very own home, it is likely to be the single largest purchasing decision you will make in your entire life. A house is more than just bricks and mortar, it's also a home. Where you live with people you love and argue with them about whose turn it is to take the bins out (ok, maybe that's just me...).

Because purchasing a home is such a significant purchase, it's vitally important that you understand what's involved and how to make good informed decisions. It might be a little sad but the average mortgage will outlast most marriages in Australia.

In this chapter, we will help you understand what's involved with purchasing your first home, from the incentives that are available to help you save a deposit, how much you are likely to need, through to what costs are involved and any other elements you should be considering when buying a house.

By the end of this chapter, you'll be better prepared for one of the biggest purchases or lifestyle decisions of your life.

Incentives

There is no doubt that getting into the housing market is proving a challenge for many these days. One of the first things you need to do is save up a deposit (or be lucky enough to be a trust-fund-kid and have millions handed to you). But for most of us, generally you'll need to save up 20% of the purchase price as well as have money set aside for related costs. It is possible to purchase a home without a 20% deposit, which we'll cover later in this chapter, but for now let's look at what you can do to save up a deposit.

If the property you want is selling for $500,000, you'll need to save up $100,000. Wow, that's a big number. Depending on how much you can set aside each pay, this can take some time. However, there are some government incentives available right now to help you get into the housing market.

First Home Super Saver Scheme
The first one is the *First Home Super Saver Scheme.* The FHSSS was introduced by the Australian Government to help people save for their first home. You can now use your super account to save for a deposit, which will help you save faster. This scheme allows you to make extra voluntary contributions from your wage into your super (either before or after tax) which you can later withdraw when you are ready to buy your first home. There are some eligibility requirements around this but the key things you need to know are:

- The FHSSS enables you to make extra contributions (on top of what your employer pays) into your super.
- You can use these extra contributions, plus the associated earnings, to help you purchase your first home. This means you may save on tax.

- The maximum you can contribute is $15,000 per financial year and $30,000 in total. These totals are per person. If you and your partner are thinking about buying a house together, you could both use this arrangement to save a combined $60,000.
- You can contribute at any age, but have to be at least 18 and not previously owned property in Australia before to access the funds.
- These funds can only be released once. So make sure you are ready to buy the house and you have saved as much as you need. Once released you have 12 months to purchase a home.
- If you don't end up using the funds to purchase a home, you can return the funds to your super, or keep them, but you'll pay a FHSSS penalty tax of 20%.

This can be a great strategy to help you save for three key reasons.

1. The money is set aside specifically for this purpose – avoids temptation.
2. It allows you to contribute your pre-tax salary meaning you will pay less tax and have more money saved.
3. The associated earnings are higher than what online savings accounts currently offer.

There is some fine print that you'll need to go over. Things like, you have to draw the money down from your super before you sign the contract on the house. So we would encourage you to have a look at the Australian taxation office website (www.ato.gov.au) for full details and to make sure you're eligible and that you use the scheme correctly.

First Home Owners Grant

Another incentive to help people get into their first house is the *First Home Owners Grant (FHOG)*. This scheme has undergone repeated changes since it was first introduced back in 2000. While the FHOG is a national scheme, it's funded by the states and territories—and administered by each of them individually. So each state or territory tweaks its own FHOG rules pretty much every year.

This means that depending on where you live, the benefits vary along with the eligibility requirements. Again, each state and territory has its own rules, but the following conditions generally apply:

- It's only available to first home buyers. You—and your spouse/partner—can't have owned property before.
- You can only receive the grant once.
- You must be an Australian citizen or permanent resident (may vary by state/territory).
- You must be a 'natural' person. In other words, a real human, not a company or a trust.
- You must live in the house for at least six months once it's built.
- Most states and territories have a minimum age requirement (usually 18).
- Maximum purchase price is between $575,000 and $750,000 (depending on state/territory).
- In almost every instance, the property must be either new or 'substantially renovated' (ie. much more than just a new kitchen).

This can provide a serious benefit so it's essential that you look into whether you can access this in your own state or territory. The rules also tend to change, so for the most up to date info, go to www.firsthome.gov.au to check out your state's eligibility requirements.

Are there any other concessions?

You'll need to check the rules for your state or territory, but you could be eligible for:

- discounts on stamp duty – some states and territories can waive or discount stamp duty up to some property price limits
- regional property concessions – you may be eligible for a larger grant if buying or building in regional areas, or even a larger discount on stamp duty.

The great news is that you aren't limited to accessing just one of these schemes, all of them can be combined to help you purchase your first home. Hooray.

The First Home Loan Deposit Scheme explained

From 1 January 2020, the government will provide a guarantee to first home buyers who have a deposit of between 5% and 20% of the property's price. This will mean they can get home loans without lenders' mortgage insurance (LMI) which is normally required for deposits below 20%.

If you've saved 5% of the purchase price of your property, the government will guarantee the remaining 15% of the deposit. You will still need to borrow 95%, but you can avoid LMI.

At the time of writing, there are still some details to be confirmed, but the aim is that this scheme will help first-home buyers get into the market earlier and at a lower cost.

The scheme will be administered through the National Housing Finance and Investment Corporation (NHFIC) in partnership with lenders. The government has announced it would prioritise "smaller lenders to boost competition". The value of eligible homes under the scheme will vary by region.

5% deposit home loans already exist, but you generally need to pay LMI when borrowing more than 80% of a property's value. The lower your deposit, the more LMI costs. This can add thousands or tens of thousands to your borrowing costs.

The First Home Loan Deposit Scheme removes this cost, so you're saving money and also time. Simply put, you can save a 5% deposit in a quarter of the time it would take to save 20%. Again, hooray.

To be eligible, you will need to be a first-home buyer (if you own an investment property, you won't be eligible). You need to be earning

$125,000 per year or less for a single, or $200,000 per year or less for a couple.

The scheme will be limited to 10,000 borrowers each year on a first-come, first-serve basis. This might seem like a big number but considering that there are about 100,000 first home buyers each year in Australia, you will need to get your skates on, to take advantage of this program.

What costs will I face when purchasing a home?

Bank fees and charges

If you have never bought a house before, you need to know that there are plenty of related costs when purchasing a home. While the purchase price is by far the biggest, you need to make sure your deposit includes money set aside for additional expenses.

A general rule of thumb is, the bigger your deposit, the better. Not only does this save you money and interest over the term of your loan, which in and of itself can be a considerable amount of money. It can also mean you'll have more options available to you when hunting for the best home loan deal. Most banks and lenders charge home loan application fees which could range from $0 to $700. Being in a good position to borrow, means getting a better deal.

If you are wanting to buy but have less than a 20% deposit, you may face lenders mortgage insurance (LMI). The title may be a little deceptive for some. When I first heard it, I thought I was paying insurance for me, just in case something happened and I couldn't pay my mortgage, I would be covered. This was and is totally incorrect.

Lenders mortgage insurance, means you are paying the insurance premium to protect the bank, so the beneficiary of the cover, is the bank, not you! What!? Don't you wish we could implement this kind of scheme in other areas of our lives, where we are the beneficiaries? I would do something like: make my vet pay for my dog's pet insurance premiums. Or make my mechanic pay for my car insurance. It's ludicrous in other industries but it is normal in banking.

And it's expensive!!!!!! The closer you borrow to 100% of the value of the house, the more expensive it becomes. For example, let's take a loan of $600,000, if you have less than 20% deposit, you could face lenders mortgage insurance of up to $24,000 which you'll have to pay up front. This is a massive amount of money and if it's possible, please do yourself a favour and avoid it. In short, the more money you can save, the less LMI you'll have to pay. If you can save 20% you'll avoid it all together.

But, what if you are keen to get into the market because the cost of renting is more than what you'd pay to service a mortgage, or the property market is rapidly rising?

Guarantor Loans

One of the ways you can avoid lenders mortgage insurance without having the full 20% deposit saved is to have a guarantor on your loan. This means that another person provides another property as security and effectively guarantees that if for any reason you are unable to meet your mortgage payments, then the bank will be able to hold that person to account. This is a serious commitment and not something to enter into lightly.

More often than not, it's parents choosing to go as guarantor to help their children purchase their first home. If your parents are wanting to help you, you may wish to have that conversation with them. But you need to know that it's also okay for them to say 'no' to this. They're taking on the risk that if something happened to you, they would take over the mortgage and they might be in a position where they either can't do that or they don't want to. They get to share the risk, you get all the benefits.

But it also doesn't have to be your parents. It could be a friend, sibling, uncle or aunt, a cousin or a business partner. You can really ask anybody. I've even seen an employer do this for one of their key employees.

If you go down this route, your lender or mortgage broker can help walk you through what's involved and it's advisable to get legal advice.

Word to the wise: If you are fortunate enough to have your parents or any other person go out on a limb for you and risk themselves financially for your benefit, you owe it to them to do everything you can to protect them. This means making sure you have comprehensive and adequate personal insurances in place. (Check out the 'Get Secure' chapter for details on this.)

Likewise, if someone asks you to be a guarantor on their mortgage, we strongly suggest you insist that they have their personal insurances professionally sorted. This will help to protect you from the financial fall out of what could be an entirely avoidable risk.

Stamp Duty

Another cost you may face when you get into the housing market is stamp duty. Stamp duty is a state-based tax and therefore differs in each state and territory. But for an example, if you bought a $600,000 home in New South Wales, the stamp duty you would be required to pay on that house purchase would be approx. $22,000. You may be exempted from stamp duty or it can be waived, deferred or discounted so it's important to do your research to make sure that you get all of your entitlements.

Legal fees

Another one-off fee that you need to be aware of is a conveyancing fee. You'll need to engage the services of a lawyer who will review your property purchase contract and assist with the transfer of ownership of the property into your name. This an upfront cost and can be anywhere from $500 to $2,200. So when you're thinking about your budget and how much you have to spend, keep that in mind.

In some states it's also mandatory to have a building & pest inspection report prepared. This is typically paid by the seller, but the cost gets passed onto the purchaser at settlement.

Other costs
If up until this point you've been living at home, or renting, there are some ongoing costs that you need to be aware of, some of which only exist when you own the property.

- Building and contents insurance
- Rates
- Utilities such as Water, Gas & Electricity
- Body corporate fees
- Ongoing maintenance of a house (most people forget to budget for this last part)

These are all pretty common, and you can talk to people who own houses about how much those things cost in your area.

Body corporate fees usually apply to units or townhouses. The body corporate is an organisation that exists in properties that share common areas. This includes things like a garden, a driveway or a pool. All these things need to be maintained and will be looked after through the body corporate. Body corporate fees really varying depending on what facilities are available. But you could be looking at anything from $2,000 to $10,000 a year. Before you commit to purchasing a property, make sure you ask the real estate agent for a report or breakdown of past body corporate fees and factor these ongoing costs into your Living Budget.

So let's say you feel that you are ready to start house hunting. What next?

Getting home loan finance
Buying a house is such a big financial commitment we recommend talking to a mortgage broker to find the best home loan deal for you. A mortgage broker's role is to have a look at your situation, your finances and compare options before recommending a suitable option for you. They will also save you the hassle when it comes to much of

the paperwork and will chase up the lender for you and guide you through the process.

Note: Get this part sorted before you make an offer on a property!

The mortgage broker gets paid by the lender when your loan settles, meaning the service is at no cost to you. You can always go direct to a lender, but they are only going to compare for you the products provided in house, and won't look elsewhere to see if you can get a better deal. Both the mortgage broker and the lender will usually be able to give you guidance on topics like the First Home Owners' Grant or any applicable stamp duty concessions.

A lender or mortgage broker is there to provide a service and tell you what you "can" do. The service rarely extends to what you "should" do. That starts to move into personal advice territory and you'll need a financial adviser who is licensed to give you advice on the "should" side of things. Some financial advisers also offer mortgage brokering services which allows them to consider both sides of the equation at the same time.

There are so many options and things you need to consider. A lender will tell you how much they're willing to lend you. It's the role of the adviser to work out how much should you really spend, taking into account any goals you have, such as plans to take time off for parental leave, or putting additional money into investments, or returning to school. Do you want the standard 30 year loan term? Or are you better off having part or all of your loan on a shorter loan term to help you commit to paying it off faster? Should you consider an interest only loan or principal and interest repayments? Should you consider fixing part or all of the home loan interest rate? If you are planning on extra repayments, should this go into a loan redraw facility or an offset account?

There are lots of things to consider. So we suggest the use of a mortgage broker who will help you get the best deal for you. If you want personal advice beyond being matched to a deal, it's best to seek the services of an adviser (check out our chapter on how to get a guru).

Once you know that you have your financial ducks all lined up in a row, you can then start seriously house hunting.

One of the reasons it's important to have your borrowing eligibility covered off depending on how you buy your house, there will be different financial requirements. For example,

Purchasing a home

If you are up for the excitement and stress of buying a house at auction, you will need to already have unconditional pre-approval on your home loan before you bid. If you don't, you risk being penalised. The person selling the house could be entitled to anything up to $20,000. You would have to pay this as a dishonour fee. So it's really important that you have pre-approval, you know your limits, and stick to your budget. Don't over commit.

If you put an offer on a house that's for sale, in the more traditional offer and purchase method, you can make your offer conditional on getting finance. Which means when you find a house that you like you can make an offer that's within your budget. This gives you a bit more time and safety as the lender will assess the value of the home. They won't automatically agree that it is worth what you are offering. If you purchase a home for $500,000 and a bank feels that the home is only worth $480,000, they'll only be willing to lend you 80% of the value which would be $384,000 rather than the full $400,000 you were expecting. This could leave you short or having to pay lenders mortgage insurance that you weren't expecting. This isn't that uncommon, but sometimes, (and certainly more rarely) the reverse can happen where the lender will value the property at a price higher than what you offered. Once your offer has been accepted and becomes unconditional, usually you have about 6 weeks before settlement occurs which is the point at which you officially purchase and become the new owner. If you need to, you can always negotiate for a shorter or longer settlement period.

You can also buy a property "off the plan", which usually means that you are purchasing a unit or townhouse in a development which hasn't yet been built. This will enable you to purchase a brand new home, based on pre-agreed plans and lists of what will be included.

It can be hard to visualise what the property will look and feel like by the time it is built and there can be delays in the build. There are literally thousands and thousands of stories of people who've been caught out where the build time experienced delays. It may not bother you as this may provide you with additional time to continue to grow your savings and a risk you are willing to take. But if you are renting and you have a firm exit date on your current living arrangements, you could find yourself in a tricky situation where you don't have any accommodation secured for a period of time. No one wins when you have to move back in with your parents for a while...

To purchase off the plan, you need to put a deposit down to secure your property with the balance being paid once the building is completed. A risk (or benefit) can be that the value of your property may fall or rise between the time you commit to purchasing and by the time the property has been built. If you experience significant changes such as losing your job, you may not be able to get finance when the property is ready to become yours. Also be careful around the quality of the build. Because you can't see it you might be buying into a building that will have structural issues and be difficult to sell in the future. No one wants to own a lame duck unit.

Lastly, another way to buy a house is to build. A key difference between this option and off the plan is that rather than paying a deposit and the balance at the end, you will make progress payments as the property is being built. More of a pay-as-you-go plan. So when the build hits certain milestones, you pay the builder progress payments. For example, the slab might be poured and then you owe the builder $20,000. Similar to off the plan, you may experience significant delays, whether it's due to poor weather or unforeseen changes such as loss of employees for the build company.

The attraction here is being able to have a home built to your own requirements, rather than choosing something pre-packaged. The downside is that if you are renting or have a mortgage on another home, as the home gets closer to completion, you are effectively paying two sets of mortgages, or both rent and a mortgage, but the benefit of only living in one property.

You can end up in quite a tight financial position while you're paying both rent and a mortgage. It still could be something that you do, but you need to take this aspect into consideration and include the dual financial commitment into your Living Budget.

Some things to think about as you're looking at what you can afford once you get into your own place. You could open it up to international students, join AirBnB, or you could rent out a spare room to help subsidise the mortgage costs.

Whatever option you go with, don't overcommit. One of the biggest mistakes is wanting your first home to be your dream home and then finding out you are painfully overcommitted and mortgage poor. Sometimes we need to be more realistic about what we can afford and downgrade our expectations. It's not forever and it doesn't mean that we won't end up in a house that we love. But there is nothing more stressful than being in a house that you love, but it limits your choices and becomes a regretful anchor. So we suggest choosing a house you can still be proud of, with the smallest loan, that gives you room for a life, while working towards your dream home.

Add to this, that at the moment, Australian interest rates are at record lows. If you want to get into the market, home loan rates have never been better, but they won't always be this low. When you are considering what repayments you can afford, you need to factor in that one-day interest rates will go back up. On a home loan of $800,000 at 3.6% the monthly repayments over a 30 year term are $3,637. Of this amount $2,400 is interest. The rest is paying back what you've borrowed.

If interest rates return to more historical averages – say 6% then your repayments would be $4,796 each month. Of this only $796 goes to paying off your loan, the rest is all interest charges. Over the life of the loan, you'd pay almost $1 million in interest charges.

If you started out with a more modest property that meant you only borrowed half this amount - $400,000, you guessed it, your repayments would be half. Meaning you can use that money in other areas of your life, whether it's: growing your wealth; being able to work part time; have longer parental leave if and when you have kids, or taking fabulous holidays each year to see the world. Point is you have choices, you could also use the spare money to smash out your home loan in record time and get to the ultimate goal of being entirely debt-free. For a more detailed look at smashing out your debts refer to our chapter, Get the Heck Out.

In summary, take advantage of the different incentives to save up for the biggest home deposit you can reasonably achieve, don't overcommit to purchasing a home just because the bank says you can, and make sure you get financial approval in place before you commit to purchasing a property. And good luck!

Renting

What if you don't want to buy a house? What if you are happy renting? There is a theory that if you don't commit to a mortgage and instead rent, you can use any money saved and invest it to make money and set you up for retirement. This might be an okay strategy in theory but most people I see that claim to be doing this aren't actually using that money for investing. They spend it here and now, on lifestyle choices. Technically there's not anything wrong with that strategy but I think you need to be really careful if that's what you decide to do and actually make sure that you invest that money wisely (check out our Get Rich chapter for investment information).

You also need to consider if you're choosing to rent long-term, the inconvenience of it. You need a bond, of course, which is usually about four weeks rent. The upside is that you won't need building insurance, rates and body corporate bills, or have to worry about repair and some maintenance costs. But renters usually move more than people who own their own home. Moving house is an experience everyone dreads and there are costs associated every time you need to move. I know a family and they were renting and due to a variety of situations, moved 13 times in 11 years, with three small children in tow. There is a real inconvenience to this, apart from the actual moving costs. There is also the secondary inconvenience like redirecting your mail, for example or potentially having to change schools.

Renting can also be inconvenient in that it can limit your availability to have pets and really make the house your home with things like hanging pictures. I know some state governments are starting to regulate more in favour of the tenant to make these kinds of things easier for people. Then there is always the dreaded inspections.

At the end of the day, if you choose to rent you will likely always need to rent. With a home, eventually you should pay it off and you'll own the asset. This will help give you security in your retirement by ensuring that you have somewhere to live and have more control over your environment.

CHAPTER 8

GET A GOOD DEAL

— $ $ $ —

Everyone wants to get ahead, right? It brings to mind images of having pole position at the traffic lights or being promoted in record time. Getting ahead, getting in front of people.

When we talk about 'getting ahead' in this chapter, it's all about finding ways to get more out of the money that you already have, whether it's getting a bargain or salary packaging to cover your goals while paying less tax. In short, making your money go further or fast track you towards your dreams and goals – whatever is most important to you.

These tips could save you thousands of dollars and help you avoid, or maybe even end your financial stress ultimately getting you what or where you want to be, sooner.

So how do you get more money? Well there are a couple of ways you can do this. You can ask for a pay raise. We covered earning more in our chapter Get More Money and we hope you have already had success in boosting your income. Regardless of whether you attempted this, or the level of your success, there are other ways you could earn some extra money.

This is all based on the theory that 'a dollar saved is a dollar earned'. If you can cut your expenses, by getting better deals, or using your money more tax effectively and making wiser purchasing decisions, or hell, you can now get something for free, then this will allow you to redirect your money to things that will improve your financial situation.

Buying a car

Let's start with cars. Many people need or want a car (whether it's a motorbike, van, truck or sedan, we'll just refer to it as a car in this chapter). After purchasing a home, a car is typically the next most significant purchase. So it's a key item to look at to see what you can do to lower the impact on your cash flow and boost your bottom line.

When you visit a car dealership, you're surrounded by shiny new cars, with that unmistakable new car smell that you want. Whether the price tag on your car is $15,000, $30,000, $50,000, $80,000 or even higher, there's no doubt it's a big purchase. Especially given that you'll probably purchase several vehicles over your lifetime.

Everybody knows that when you buy a brand new car, the moment you drive it out of the car yard it is worth less than what you paid for it, and the resale value continues to decline as the years roll on. It's a depreciating asset, in that while the cost of almost everything else goes up, from housing to a loaf of bread over time, the resale value of your car drops every year. But few people realise how fast a car loses its value. As a general rule of thumb, a car will lose 50% of its resale value in the first three years of its life.

So that $50,000 car you bought may now only be worth $25,000 after only three years of driving (and that's without accidents or things like hail damage affecting the value). The car still has the same functionality to you. It still drives pretty well. Most warranties these days, often offer five, six or even seven years with unlimited kilometres, meaning it is still a good and reliable car despite the loss in value.

But let's be real here, anything that loses 50% of its value in 3 years is a bad investment when you know there won't be any change in the direction of its value. You'd be crazy to throw that kind of money away with any other area of your life, so why do it with a car when you don't have to?

There will always be people who buy brand-new cars even when they know it's a massive drain on their finances, so let's let those people waste their money and depreciate the car for us. Maybe they have the money to waste? Or perhaps it's their vice. Whatever their reason, it can benefit you.

Katherine: I have only once in my life purchased a brand-new car and honestly, in the end, I regretted my decision. Nowadays, whenever I purchase a car I look for something that is maybe two or three years old (thankful somebody else depreciated the car for me with their money) while I can still get the benefit of the warranties.

So, let's say I want a car that would be $50,000 to buy brand new. I find it difficult to justify spending $50,000 on a car when I know it means I'll likely be throwing half of that money away before too long. I have two options in front of me. I can purchase the model of car I want by buying a car that is 2 - 4 years old and while I know it will still drop in value, the steepest part is over and less of my money will be wasted and I can probably buy the car for $25,000 to $35,000. Or if I am prepared to spend $50,000, I can get a top of the line car that I would likely never consider being in my price range because it may have cost $100,000 when it was brand new.

Here's another thing when it comes to purchasing a car. You will save yourself thousands of dollars if you can purchase a car outright. Why is this? Well if you don't have the money saved up, you'll have to borrow money whether it's against your mortgage, a car loan or dealer finance. Whatever option you choose to organise a loan, it means that not only will you have the purchase price of the car to repay, but also the interest on the loan. Interest rates can vary, but let's assume you've borrowed $40,000 to purchase a car at an interest rate of 7% on a five-year loan term.

Assuming no loan fees, over the 5 years your monthly repayments will add up to $47,523 before you manage to pay it off. The monthly loan repayments commit you to $792 each month.

But wait, home loan interest rates are so low right now, what if you just borrow against your home? Home loan interest rates are lower, but most people make two mistakes, they refinance their home loan and in the process usually re-set the home loan term to 30 years, and then repay their car loan over this period. If you were to borrow $40,000 via this alternative at an interest rate of 3.75% you may think this is a good deal as your loan repayments are a much lower $185 each month, but over the life of the loan your total repayments add up to a whopping $66,689.

If you choose to borrow using your home loan to purchase a car, consider having a separate loan with a short term, otherwise it will cost you more. Furthermore, as you're unlikely to keep your car for 30 years, you'll struggle to pay off your mortgage as you may find yourself paying off multiple car loans for cars you no longer have.

Weirdly, many people have very few concerns about committing to a car loan and are happy to plug the loan repayments into their budget, as this just seems like the normal thing to do. But many people are very resistant to the idea of saving up tens of thousands of dollars to be able to pay for their car in cash. If you do it this way, once you've purchased a car, instead of car loan repayments, you can start putting money aside each paycheck for your next car. If you break the cycle and do it this way, you'll be earning interest on your savings, rather than paying it on your loan.

The lesson here is that it's not just the purchase price, when you borrow money, it's also the interest on the loan repayments. You might be increasing the purchase price by a staggering 65% or more, then years later wonder why you never seem to be able to get ahead.

Even if you don't have all of the money you need to buy a car outright, make an effort to borrow as little as possible by using savings and avoid buying a brand new car. This will free up your cash-flow so you can get ahead and do more life changing stuff with your money.

What if I can salary package a car? I've heard it is a better way to purchase a car. If you need to purchase a car, being able to salary package a vehicle can make it a little more affordable as the tax benefits may save you a few thousand dollars each year. But for most people, it's one of the worst traps.

The line you get sold on is 'well you'll be using pre-tax dollars which is a cheaper way of purchasing the car.' Well, yes, it can lower the cost of buying a car. But it won't lower it as much as not having to borrow the money in the first place. It is possible to purchase a second hand car this way, with some restrictions such as the car has to be only a few years old (totally workable), but most people use these arrangements to purchase a brand-new car, and unlike a personal loan, once you have finished your salary packaging term, you don't own the car outright, there is always a residual loan (usually called a balloon payment) at the end that you owe. Rather than having this money ready to go, the car gets sold and it's usually just enough to repay the balloon payment at the end and the cycle starts all over again. It becomes a perpetual cycle of committing to loan repayments that lower your take home pay and never owning a car at the end of it. The tax savings of a few thousand each year pale in comparison to the tens of thousands of dollars you are throwing away by keeping this cycle on repeat.

But what if you have to buy a car and you want a salary package? If you weigh up the different options and at the end of the day decide that salary packaging looks like a good option for you, for the love of God, at the end of the term, keep the car. Choose a car that is near new (but not brand new). Don't go and sell it and then repeat the process and get another packaged car. All you are doing is throwing away your money and living in perpetual debt. When the salary packaging companies offer this as an option, they know the principles that we talked about earlier; people budget, based on their bank accounts. So, with this money being taken out of your pre-tax earnings, you adjust and just get used to living on the leftover pay packet. You are essentially committing to a lower wage. But if you didn't have to package that car, or better yet, pay any car loan at all, you could have significantly more money coming into your pay account. Car loans don't have to be an ongoing expense in your Spending Plan (honestly the running costs alone are enough).

If you're planning to package a vehicle, the priority has to be that you will have enough money saved to pay off the residual loan/balloon payment and work out how much you will need to set aside each pay in a separate account to ensure you have enough when the term ends and include this in your Spending Plan. Once you own the car outright, aim to keep the car for at least 10 years. The way cars are built these days with good, long warranties a new car should last at least 10 years if not longer before running into expensive maintenance. This will save you bucketloads. Enough about cars, what about other items...

Mobile Phones

Another thing people regularly upgrade, is their mobile phone. Now, full disclosure, we must admit this is something that we've both been guilty of for a long time. We love having the latest iPhone. It makes us happy. We aren't lining up outside the Apple store the day of release or anything, but the moment our mobile phone contracts comes to an end, we upgrade to the latest iPhone. We have small children, whilst we love to upgrade our phones, we're also pretty certain that we would be top contenders in the running to win some kind of award for the world's most dropped phone. So sometimes it's out of sheer desperation rather than love, despite the amount of cases that get used (and subsequently broken) while defending the life of the phone.

Katherine: In recent years we've both been really trying to get better at looking after our mobile phones. Recently, when my contract came up instead of upgrading the phone and automatically renewing the contract, I did something radical and I read the phone contract. I reckon you can do this too. One of the drivers for this was that I wasn't happy with the coverage I was getting on the network I was with (I won't say which network). I knew that Telstra's coverage was good but I just had this thing that I didn't want to deal with Telstra. In the past, I had wasted too many hours of my life when part of my job was to try and sort out problems, via a call centre, on behalf of my employer.

So, what to do when I wanted Telstra coverage but didn't want to actually have a contract with them....???? I looked a little further afield and found that Aldi (yep the grocery place) had a mobile phone plan which uses Telstra's network. The cost was much less then I was currently paying. My phone plan went from almost $100 a month plus an extra $10 per 1gb if you went over within the month which I would do semi regularly, to a pay as you go with ALDI at $25 a month and my data allowance almost tripled. Now this plan and provider might not be a great match for your needs, but my point is to check out who else is in the market, apart from the usual teleco companies, and see if there is another provider and deal that could work for you. If you can get more for less, you'd be crazy not to check it out when you can. The amount of money I'm saving means that I could now upgrade my phone almost every year, rather than every 2 years, but for me, I'll just pocket the difference and make sure I have money set aside to buy a new phone when I need to. Funnily enough, knowing that when I next upgrade my phone I'll have to fork out for it to buy it outright, it makes me want to take care of my phone better and have it last longer. Even knowing I'm better off, there's a little part of me that doesn't want to part with that money in one hit, so it works twice as well in making me think twice about how often I upgrade and saves me money.

Amber: I was a little different in that I was not using my phone plan very well. I was paying for a whole lot of data with my provider but I was using the Wi-Fi network at work and home. There are so many Wi-Fi networks available, even your local McDonald's will have free Wi-Fi. I simply didn't need to be paying for lots of data that I wasn't actually using. This meant I could opt for a lower plan and save a tonne of money in the process.

Sometimes people think that if you are a loyal customer and remain with a provider for a long period of time (whether it's a phone company, or a car/home insurance provider), that they will look after you and give you a good price for your loyalty. Unfortunately, the reverse is often true. It's often referred to as the "lazy tax". The biggest discounts often go towards attracting new customers, so don't let complacency cost you money.

Food & Groceries

Katherine: I often joke that it was because of Aldi I was able to purchase my first home. Both my husband and I were working full-time and we were struggling to save up a deposit in our desired time frame. The one thing he wouldn't compromise on is the types of food we buy. He works out a lot, and eats plenty of nuts, berries, meats including seafood and greens. His dedication to his health is something that I love about him, the impact on our Living Budget, less so. He was adamant that he didn't want to compromise on the quality of the food that we purchased. I was juggling a massive food bill but this is something that was important to him. I had heard about Aldi but was nervous to try it, thinking there would be lots of brands that I didn't know or recognise and thought the odds were I'd be committing to two grocery shops and let's face it, I didn't want to change. But I was desperate to change the amount we were spending on groceries and decided to give it a go. Honestly, going into the store for the first time, I was overwhelmed. Nothing looked the way I was used to, and the aisles were all laid out in a different way and I thought 'how can I possibly find everything in this place.' I picked up a couple of items that required minimal mental workload and left the store as quickly as I could and didn't think I would really go back. But the products I did buy, I actually really liked, so I decided to give it another go. The next time I went in, I decided to go with a list of things that I would always buy on my normal grocery run. I was determined to find those items, knowing that they wouldn't be in the same packaging or aisle location that I was used to. To my surprise, I managed to find about 80% of the things that I would normally buy on my list. That was enough to keep me going back over the next couple of months. As I did my grocery shops, I managed to find the remaining items I couldn't find the first times I went. They were there all along. I just didn't realise it. It got to the point where there were only two things that I wanted to buy that I couldn't find and had to source from elsewhere.

The savings for our family were massive. I went from spending a whopping $400 a fortnight (for two adults) to less than $200 a fortnight. This was for the same groceries without compromising on quality and I was able to slash my grocery bill in half. This money we saved went into our first home saving account and helped us purchase our first home that much sooner.

Even though most people know that Aldi offers a significantly better bang for your buck when it comes to groceries, most Australians still shop at Coles and Woollies. If you are serious about saving money, give shopping at Aldi a go and if you're already doing it, you know what I'm talking about when I say the quality is good and the prices are great. I know it's different and that middle aisle is always full of the strangest stuff (who doesn't want to buy a chainsaw with your cheese and cucumber???) but the savings are worth a little bit of weirdness. If money doesn't motivate you, I've also found that Aldi seems to use less preservatives, additives, artificial colourings and the like in their products and source a higher portion of their produce from Australia. Double win!

In fact, since July 2018, Aldi has the highest net promoter score of all the grocery chains, meaning it is the most trusted and likely to be recommended by its customers. Aside from grocery chains, it's now the most trusted brand in Australia. Yet, the majority of consumers shop at the two largest chains, Woolworths and Coles.

Full disclosure: I'm also a just a wee bit competitive and while some people are a little bit daunted by the need to pack their own groceries into their own bags and trolley, as a former check out chick (many moons ago) I love the challenge of impressing the cash register operator of how fast I can pack my groceries! Weird, but that's me. But these days I struggle to stand in line at a "normal" grocery store line watching an operator pack bags at a snail's pace, and don't get me started when it comes to walking into a large grocery aisle and having to choose between 23 varieties of tomato sauce. Not only do I save money, but I feel like I do my brain a favour by making my decisions so much simpler. Decision fatigue is real my friends and I don't want to waste what precious brain capacity I have on the weekend in the grocery aisle.

There are also other options out there too such as supporting local farmers and buying in bulk or via food co-ops, or growing your own items, particularly expensive items such as berries. The aim here is to spend less, without giving up on quality or having to do without and we think that taking the time to familiarise yourself with alternative ways of sourcing your groceries and household goods is worth the time. Your wallet will thank you!

Travel

We love holidays here at Money Madams and we love a good deal. Getting a good deal on a holiday is a great thing. One of the most frustrating things about travel is that the most convenient times to travel are usually the most expensive. Christmas, Easter, school holidays and over summer. Demand is higher and with it prices go up on just about everything. Everyone is travelling right? And one of the most expensive elements of a holiday is the accommodation. Well what if instead of being penalised with higher prices, with a few simple changes you could use the fact that everyone is travelling to be in your favour?

Over these busy periods, house sitters are in high demand. They may have a pet that they can't take with them when they are travelling or just want the peace of mind knowing someone is in their house and it's not sitting vacant. So instead of paying for accommodation at peak season prices, why not look into housesitting in the location you want to travel to. For example, you want to go to the Gold Coast for Christmas and New Year's and you don't want to pay exorbitant rates in peak season. Instead why not jump on online notice-boards and offer to house sit for a local while you are in town. It's a win-win. You get free accommodation and the homeowner gets someone reliable to look after their house while they are away. Amber has done this over Christmas one year. She was travelling back to her parents' house for Christmas and needed someone to look after her dog for a few weeks. On her work notice board there was someone who was moving to Canberra to start work at the same employer and was looking for short term accommodation while he and his family settled into a new city. He also happened to be a vet (you don't get much better if you are looking for a dog sitter!) It was a win-win for both of them (although possibly not for the dog. He doesn't like his trips to the vet usually, so perhaps living with one was not his idea of a holiday).

So, if you are after free accommodation in peak season have a look around for house sitting gigs. The earlier you start looking the better your chances are of finding your dream location and dates. You might have to be flexible with the exact dates but do a good job, get some references and you could set yourself up for super cheap holidays for years!!! In fact, some people go so far as to line up house sitting gigs for months and live rent and mortgage free within their home city to help them save up for a home deposit. If you are interested, there are loads of websites and networks that link potential house sitters with people looking for them.

Another alternative is to take tag team vacations. What's that you ask? Well this is an idea that works well for parents who need a little R & R or you and your partner find it difficult to agree on where to spend your holiday dollars. In short it works like this. Instead of holidaying with your partner, you have a holiday with a friend. The benefit is that it is half the cost to your household Living Budget as you only pay for one person's flight (or go halves on the fuel), share the accommodation costs etc. It's a great opportunity to catch up on quality time with long forgotten friends and if you are a parent, leave your kids at home with your partner, and have yourself a mum-cation where you recharge your batteries and have a little you time. This means you may also be able to travel to locations where the distance, location or activities may not be suitable for young children.

Of course it's a tag team deal so you and your partner would take it in turns. This idea was inspired by Amber. When Amber's babies were small, Rowan flew to Africa to help support some communities over there as part of the church group. Later, Amber found herself being invited to Paris to spend time with a friend. Well, Amber was due a Mum-cation by this time and the idea was born. We got our husbands officially on board with the idea. It was easy to convince them when we suggested they should travel the first year making it hard for them to refuse when it was our turn. Not long after, they were off to Nepal together and making their way to Base camp on Mt Everest (Amber did not have the shoes required for this trek and I have no desire to go either). But by sending our husbands off together, they got to do something they had always wanted to do, it was significantly cheaper just to send one person in the household and they came back refreshed and excited, ready to spend more time and energy with the family.

We do have some rules around these holidays. You can't go somewhere the other person is desperate to go and we have limits on the budget and time away from the family. But the benefits are real. It enriches our marriage as we support our partners in fulfilling their dreams. It's not the only holidays we take. We certainly also take breaks and go away all together, kids included. But these tag team holidays are special. It has become a great way to take international holidays without breaking the bank and catching up with friends.

Debt

What about saving money in other areas. What about your home loan? Well even if you have a home loan already it pays to shop around!!! If you have a fixed rate loan, we don't fancy your chances of renegotiating your interest rate or being able to leave for another provider without being slugged a fee, but if you are on a variable rate, it's worth calling your bank and say:

- I'm a loyal customer and I'm happy here but I have had a look around and I've noticed that if I go to "insert name here" bank, I can get a better deal where the offer is "details of competitor's offer" (make sure it is a real deal someone else is offering).

- I'm tempted to move but would be prepared to stay with you if you could do me a deal. Can you put me through to the loan retention team so I can decide whether they can make it worth my while to stay, or whether I should leave for a competitor's deal.

Most banks want to keep you as a customer, so they will probably offer you a deal to improve your home loan rate. If they are unwilling to negotiate, and a competitor has a much better deal, it could be worth your while to move banks. Some people are put off by the inconvenience of changing loan providers, and sometimes just calling your bank to let them know that you are thinking of moving but would like to stay with them, is enough to get a better deal. But if it's not, and they can't offer you something to stay, then maybe it is time that you move on.

Home loans are expensive and even saving a small amount on your interest rate can save you thousands over the long run. There are other factors to consider beyond the interest rate such as offset accounts, redraw facilities, access to fee free banking products, and other fees and charges you may incur such as loan application and discharge fees etc. But generally speaking, the bigger your loan, the bigger the impact will be on your wallet by accessing a lower interest rate.

If you have a mortgage of $500,000, reducing your mortgage interest rate by 0.25% will save you approximately $25,640 over a 30 year loan term. If you can't get the interest rate you want, and you don't want the hassle of changing banks, consider asking for other options such as having fees waived where possible on bank accounts or other services.

We know that moving banks can be inconvenient, however, it's worth it if it means saving thousands!!!

Getting a bargain on general purchases

We all know that it's better to purchase something on sale rather than pay full price. But here at Money Madams we love to stretch our dollar as far as it goes and buy second hand bargains too. One of Katherine's favourite things to do is go to the Boxing Day sales every year. Everyone loves a bargain. Now she doesn't just go to the sales and to get caught up in the frenzy. She goes prepared. She saves up any gift cards or vouchers she has been given from family and friends. She also plans what she needs and hunts out those things. It's fun to buy things on sale but don't get so caught up that you buy things you don't really need. That's not a bargain but we all know people who this has happened to right?

Some people take it too far and they get caught up in the frenzy of purchasing a good deal because it's on sale, not because they really want it. So, we find that in the weeks after Christmas and Boxing Day sales, there is plenty of buyers remorse going around and a bucketload of bargains to be found. The prime locations being sites like eBay, Facebook marketplace and Gumtree.

People have purchased clothing, shoes and other items only to realise that they don't like the way it sits on them, or it's the wrong size or they just have buyer's remorse and they can't take it back to the retailer as the item was purchased on sale. It's in perfect condition. They can't get the price they bought it for because now that it's no longer a brand-new item, people simply aren't willing to pay the same price the retailer is charging for it. So you can snag an item that is still brand new, but now discounted even further.

We do look at my local Facebook page or eBay and find those items that people have regretted purchasing and get an even cheaper price than what they paid for the item. Our preference is Gumtree or Facebook marketplace over eBay, simply because we can actually go and physically see the item and try it on before deciding whether to buy it. You also don't have to pay for postage and can get the item on the spot. You will be amazed at what you can find on these sites year round, but especially early in the new year. Whether it's clothing, furniture, appliances or toys.

Most of these people selling don't have credit card facilities. This is another reason why having cash ready to go means you can get better deals to seize opportunities, to save even more money.

So, don't just buy things on places like eBay and Facebook marketplace or gumtree, sell things as well. There will be items in your life that have a limited season whether you like following the latest fashion trends or not. If you no longer need a piece of furniture or there is a piece of gym equipment that you promised yourself that you would use but you don't, or your children no longer need their baby clothes or baby furniture, or they have outgrown certain toys, sell the stuff. Rather than just throwing it away, you may find a buyer on one of these sites. It'll do two things for you:

First, the most obvious one is that you get some money that you wouldn't have otherwise.

Secondly, it's a little effort but makes you more conscious about what you are spending money on and shifts the focus to sustainability and giving items a second life.

A good rule of thumb is when one thing comes in, one thing goes out.

As you buy a new dress, sell an old dress. It helps you make more conscious decisions about what you are buying and if you really want it, helps keep your wardrobe under control and the money you make can discount the new purchase. You can avoid items that you don't really need.

Small ideas that add up

It pays to also think outside the box to lower your costs. We know two girls who realised that they were spending far too much money on takeaway lunches each week. But the commitment of having to prepare lunches every single day in order to save themselves from buying takeout just simply felt exhausting. They came up with a deal that they would take it on turns to make each other lunch. And they would have their takeaway meal just one day per week. So, one would cook her dinner on a Sunday night and cook up enough that she could pack two lunches to take to work for herself and a friend on Monday. Then it would be her friend's turn to do the same thing but she cooked it on Monday night, for Tuesday. It was not a lot more effort because they were cooking dinner anyway (not packing a separate lunch) and even then, they only had to do it twice a week and managed to cut back their spending on takeaway lunches from five days a week to just one.

On Friday, as a way of celebrating, they both went out and had lunch together. This was saving them about $50 a week each. That adds up to a couple of thousand dollars per year. And not only that, they got to enjoy somebody else's cooking and the commitment of knowing that they had a friend counting on them meant they didn't opt out and change their mind at the last minute because it would be rude to cancel (so added a level of accountability as well).

Also make sure that you're not paying fees that you don't have to be paying. That means bank accounts, even things like paying a bill by Bpay, may incur a fee versus a direct debit. Check the way you are getting statements. Sometimes getting electronic statements can save you money and they charge you a fee to send you out a paper statement. Just like calling up your home loan lender to negotiate a better deal, don't forget you can apply this same technique to your car insurance, your home and contents insurance and any other service that you are using. Check subscriptions and make sure you are using everything you are paying for. Find ways to cut costs and getting a better deal. It all adds up.

CHAPTER 9

GET THE HECK OUT (OF DEBT)

$ $ $

Debt more often than not, is not a good thing. If you can avoid it, don't go into debt. Being debt free is a great goal to have (and one we should all be working towards) but unless you are a trust-fund kid, sooner or later you're probably going to borrow money. Whether it is to purchase your first car, you take out a credit card, you buy your first home, or perhaps you even decide to borrow money to invest.

No one really likes being in debt, but it's a useful tool to get you something that you may need, or that you want, right now. So, for most of us some amount of debt is inevitable. This chapter is here to give you some strategies to help you pay off your debts in the shortest time possible, as well as to help you to avoid overcommitting and falling into a situation of debt stress in the first place. If you are in debt stress, these tips will get you back into balance, which can free you up to spend money on the things that are more important. Paying off debt faster than you need to will save you a ton of money in the long term so you can enjoy the things in life that matter most to you.

There are lots of different types of debt out there. But you've probably heard the terms "good" debt and "bad" debt. So what is the difference between 'good debt' and 'bad debt'?

Good debt is money that you have borrowed and have spent on something that is likely to make you money whether it is something that will increase in value, generate income for you or a combination of both. Typical examples are things like investment property loans, business loans or loans where the money is invested in shares and other assets. The upside is that the interest on these loans are generally tax deductible because they are being used to produce investment returns that will in turn get taxed. To be sure you are claiming any and all tax deductions correctly, always seek the advice of a qualified accountant.

Bad debt is money that you have borrowed and have spent on something that will decrease in value or gets spent on consumables leaving you nothing to show for your money over the longer term. Typical examples are using credit cards to pay for things like regular household bills where you don't have the money set aside already to pay off the card in full at the end of the month, borrowing money for holidays, or cars are all examples of bad debts.

What about borrowing money to purchase a home. We don't really consider this to be a good or a bad debt, it's more a functional debt. Generally speaking, your home will go up in value, but it's not an investment that's producing an income and the interest charges aren't likely to be tax deductible, but it does serve a purpose of ensuring you have somewhere to live instead of paying rent.

Buying your first home is one of the biggest purchases that you will ever make and probably one of the biggest debts you'll ever take on. Even if you have limited spare cashflow to make extra repayments, there are a couple of tips and tricks you can apply which will save you money and reduce the term of your loan.

A simple step is to ensure that your loan comes with an offset account. An offset account is a separate transactional account that is linked to your mortgage. Any funds that sit within your offset account will reduce the amount of interest that you are charged on your loan each month. You won't actually receive an interest credit into your offset account. So why is this so good?

Let's say for example, you have a $500,000 home loan and are being charged at an interest rate of 5%. You also have an offset account and it has an account balance of $50,000. When the bank works at how much interest to charge you for that loan, they are going to take into account anything that is in the offset account and "offset" the interest you would otherwise have to pay on your mortgage. So in this example, you would only pay interest on your mortgage as if you only owed the bank $450,000. This would save you almost $100 a fortnight ($2,500 each year to be exact).

This is good for two reasons. The first is that mortgage interest rates are always higher than the interest rate that you can get on a day-to-day or online savings account. And secondly, any interest that you earn on your savings account or a high interest account is money that you have to declare as income and you will be taxed on this, which effectively reduces the benefit. With an offset account you will save yourself the mortgage interest amount (in this example 5%) and as the saying goes, 'a dollar saved, is a dollar earned' and you get to keep the entire benefit of the saving, no sharing with the tax man required.

Now, not every bank offers an offset account but usually the offset account is available to people with variable-rate loans. If you have a fixed rate loan there's a couple of restrictions for the privilege and this usually means that you don't get an offset account, or you are limited in how many extra payments you are able to make on the loan each year. Each bank will have their own rules so it's best to get it checked out with a particular bank or go through a mortgage broker who can investigate these options for you.

Another tip is to make your loan repayments fortnightly rather than monthly. Let's assume once again that you have a loan of $500,000 and your interest rate is 5%. The repayments over a 30 year loan term are $2,684 each month. If you halve this amount ($1,342) and make the repayments fortnightly instead of monthly, you'll shave almost five years off your loan term and save yourself more than $86,000 in the process. The reason this works is that each month (except February) has a little more than two fortnights. Over the course of the year you'll end up making an extra repayment and this makes a massive difference over the life of your loan.

These two simple tips require nothing or only a little extra from your day-to-day cashflow.

Let's say you don't want to take any chances and you are determined to pay off your mortgage in 20 years instead of the standard 30 year loan term. What should you be doing?

Simple! Don't take the standard 30-year loan term when you arrange your loan. Insist on a 20-year loan term. You can request a shorter loan term and it doesn't have to be the standard 30 years. The bank will of course be looking at your savings history and budget to assess whether they think this is feasible for you. Assuming that they are happy to give you a 20 year loan, and you feel comfortable that your Living Budget can commit to the higher level of repayments, do it! This way when interest rates change your loan repayments will be adjusted by the bank to keep you on schedule for your mortgage end date.

Just about everyone at one time has the inspiration to pay off their mortgage faster and they make extra payments to their loan every single week, fortnight or month. However, often these extra repayments build-up in their account and then a day comes along where they say "Gosh, we've been working so hard, wouldn't it be really good to.... "*insert shiny distraction that derails your mortgage repayment goal here*".... Whether it's an updated kitchen, buying a new car, going on a holiday.... It is something that is NOT the goal of paying off a home loan fast. Sometimes it isn't even big expenses, it can be going a little overboard on your spending and finding that you need to take money from your offset account, or your loan redraw, to cover the shortfall in your day-to-day spending. Having access to these extra repayments and the temptation that comes with that, is too much for some people and that sees them come undone.

When you have a shorter loan term, the money is being locked away and goes straight onto the principal of your loan, so it forces you to stick to your goal, make the payments and pay off the loan. Now 20 years or so is a really long time and it can feel like you aren't making much progress on your mortgage. So we have a tip to help keep you motivated when those 20 years feel like forever.

Break Up Your Loan! Breaking your loan up into two separate loans, a large chunk and a smaller one can help you to dupe yourself into feeling and staying more motivated. A good split to begin with is about 90% and 10% but choose something that works for you and the size of your loan.

To keep it simple we're going to stick with the same example of having a mortgage of $500,000. So a 90-10 split in this case would be a larger loan of $450,000 that you would pay off over the normal 30 years and a smaller loan of $50,000 which you pay off ultra-fast (say over 5 years).

The repayments in this case are pretty similar to having your whole loan on a 20 year loan term. But having a single mortgage can make your repayments feels like a drop in the ocean, only paying off a little bit extra and time moves slowly, but when you have a second smaller loan you see your balance dropping rapidly and you get that smaller amount down to say $10,000 or less, the motivation to see that loan repaid in full increases because you can see that goal getting closer. The success drives you to more success and you get motivated to pay it off even faster. It's really simple and it works!

Once that smaller loan is gone, and depending on your circumstances at the time, repeat the cycle of refinancing the loan and setting up your loan term again so that you have another smaller amount on a shorter term. Do it all again and pay your loan off in chunks. The success of being able to chomp away at your loan will see you continue to do this. Now this is no different to having a larger loan and making the additional repayments. The reason why this works is because the psychology of seeing that small loan reduce breeds success and you can't redraw the money.

The drawback can be that this money is locked away, but it's also the point. So make sure that you are comfortable and able to commit to the required repayments.

Mistakes to avoid with your mortgage

One of the biggest mistakes I see people make when they go shopping for a better mortgage deal is that they find a loan which has a lower interest rate which will shave 0.1% or 0.25% off the interest rate. But in reality, they've probably done themselves a disservice.

Let's say you've had your mortgage for five years and have decided it's time to get a better rate. You go out and find a great deal and you get your loan all set up with a new lower rate. Your rates are lower, your payments are lower and you've got more cash to do things... winning..... right?

But the reality may be that you have locked in another 30-year loan term, but before you made the switch you were five years into your last loan. You had 25 years left to repay that loan. The repayments have dropped, partly due to the lower rate, but it's also because you are stretching out the time it will take to repay the loan, which means you'll end up paying more interest over the long term which defeats the whole point of the exercise. If you had never changed a thing, you would have had that loan paid off in 25 years, now it could take you 30 years.

We're all for getting a better deal on your mortgage, but the mistake happens with the loan term.

Definitely get yourself a better deal on your mortgage. But if you go out and refinance your loan, choose a loan term that's going to ensure that you pay off your home loan when you need or want to have it paid off. And be prepared for the bank to try and talk you into a longer loan term. They will say things like *"you'll have more flexibility if you take the longer term. You can make extra payments if you want to, but the longer term and lower repayments mean you will have more money and more flexibility."* Don't fall for it. If you want to pay your loan off in a certain amount of time and you can afford to, set a shorter loan term and you will definitely pay it off in that time. Or at the very least when you change your loan, whatever years you had left on your old mortgage (in this example 25 years) choose that as the loan term with the new provider who is offering the better deal.

This brings us to talk about the two types of loans, interest only versus principal plus interest loans.

Principal plus interest loans means that the bank will charge you interest for the privilege of having a loan, but part of your repayment will pay off the principal (money off your actual loan) each month and it's amazing how small this amount actually is. This is why it takes you such a long time to pay off the loan.

An **interest only** loan is like you are renting a house. You own this property (with a mortgage interest) but you are effectively renting your home from the bank because you are not paying down the debt (the principal). While it's less than ideal, it can be a really useful strategy, but it's certainly not a permanent solution. There could be seasons in your life where money can become tight. A perfect example of this is when a couple both working full-time, decide to start a family and as part of having kids one or both of them takes time off work or reduces their work hours. Even if they both go back to work they may need to pay for childcare expenses and a whole host of new expenses. In short, things can start to get expensive and you need some cash-flow relief.

One way of managing these expenses is to take a loan from the standard principal and interest repayments and then make it an interest only loan. This will give you a little bit of extra cash flow to manage the new expenses, but it is only ever a temporary solution and you won't be paying off the loan. There's always going to be new expenses to battle so if you can, try to avoid doing this, but if you need the extra cash flow, it's an option. Just be aware that these days interest only loans typically charge a higher rate of interest and banks are not as keen on offering these loans compared to the more typical principal and interest loans.

So, what about using the equity in your home to purchase other assets like a car or to consolidate credit card debt? On the surface it seems to be a no brainer, because if you were to arrange a personal loan to borrow the money for a car, or leave your credit cards where they are, it would be at a much higher interest rate than if you were to use the equity in your home. Here's the deal: Yes, when you borrow money from your home loan, you'll get a much lower interest rate but let's look at the figures. We've covered the example of paying for a car using your home equity in the chapter "Get a Good Deal" so we'll focus on credit cards in the example below.

Let's say you have $20,000 worth of credit card debt and you are being charged 24% p.a. in interest. That's $4,800 per year in interest charges ($400 per month) before you even begin to start paying off the money you owe. Ouch!

Now if you look at consolidating a $20,000 credit card debt into your mortgage, it would mean you were paying much lower interest rates (say 5%). The increase to your loan repayments would be a much more manageable $107 each month. At this point you are feeling the relief. But the kicker is in the loan term. By paying 5% over 30 years, it will take $38,651 in repayments before it's eventually repaid. Consolidating credit cards into your mortgage only works if you use the lower interest rate and ensure the debt is paid out over a short amount of time such as a few years at the most.

If you can avoid it, don't draw down on the equity of your mortgage to consolidate debt. It's usually a symptom of a budgeting problem and unless addressed, you'll repeatedly find yourself with ever increasing credit card debt that ultimately prevents you from ever paying off your mortgage and getting ahead. If consolidating debt is unavoidable, make as much additional payments on your mortgage as you can until that debt is gone. Otherwise you could end up worse off!

In short, personal debt will not serve you well into your future. It can slow you down from reaching your dreams and goals. Thankfully there are things we can do to get rid of it. Just because you have debt now does not mean that you will have it forever. There is sometimes shame and guilt associated with personal debt. Getting rid of it not only helps your finances, it helps you feel better too.

So what do you do if you have personal debt? If you've got a lot of personal debt scattered all over the place, for example, credit cards, personal loans, car loans or even multiple ones of each of these, it can all feel really overwhelming. So where do you start? How do you start tackling your debts?

There are two popular methods; The Debt Avalanche and the Debt Snowball methods.

Both methods start out the same in that they require that you list out your debts and make only the minimum payments on all of your debts except for one.

The difference lies in which debt you tackle first.

Debt avalanche method: You focus all of your extra repayments on the debt with the highest rate of interest. Once that debt is paid off, you move onto the debt with the next highest rate of interest. This will save you the most amount of money in interest charges.

Debt snowball method: You start with the smallest debt first and work your way up, regardless of interest rate. This gives you some early wins and keeps you motivated with your success.

Imagine that you have the following debts:

- $8,000 ABC credit card debt at 24.00% (min repayment $200 pm)
- $5,000 XYZ credit card debt at 18.00% (min repayment $105 pm)
- $10,000 car loan at 7.00% (min repayment $200 pm)
- $2,000 interest-free store loan (assume 18 months remaining and min repayment of $40 pm)

You owe $25,000 in total and your combined minimum repayments are $545 each month. Let's say you have an additional $1,000 each month which you can use to help smash out your debts.

If you were following the avalanche method, you would pay off your debts in the order listed above as they are listed in the order of the highest interest rate first. This would save you $11,809 in interest charges compared to making the minimum repayments only.

The chart below shows how this would work in practice.

Month #	Credit Card ABC	Credit Card XYZ	Car Loan	Interest free deal	Total monthly repayment
1	$1,200.00	$105.00	$200.00	$40.00	$1,545.00
2	$1,200.00	$105.00	$200.00	$40.00	$1,545.00
3	$1,200.00	$105.00	$200.00	$40.00	$1,545.00
4	$1,200.00	$105.00	$200.00	$40.00	$1,545.00
5	$1,200.00	$105.00	$200.00	$40.00	$1,545.00
6	$1,200.00	$105.00	$200.00	$40.00	$1,545.00
7	$1,200.00	$105.00	$200.00	$40.00	$1,545.00
8	$273.71	$1,031.29	$200.00	$40.00	$1,545.00
9		$1,305.00	$200.00	$40.00	$1,545.00
10		$1,305.00	$200.00	$40.00	$1,545.00
11		$1,305.00	$200.00	$40.00	$1,545.00
12		$21.55	$1,483.45	$40.00	$1,545.00
13			$1,505.00	$40.00	$1,545.00
14			$1,505.00	$40.00	$1,545.00
15			$1,505.00	$40.00	$1,545.00
16			$1,505.00	$40.00	$1,545.00
17			$1,058.04	$486.96	$1,545.00
18				$873.04	$873.04

If you were following the Snowball method you would pay off the interest free loan first as it is the smallest. The chart below shows how this different approach would work in practice.

Month #	Interest free deal	Credit Card XYZ	Credit Card ABC	Car Loan	Total monthly repayment
1	$1,040.00	$105.00	$200.00	$200.00	$1,545.00
2	$960.00	$185.00	$200.00	$200.00	$1,545.00
3		$1,145.00	$200.00	$200.00	$1,545.00
4		$1,145.00	$200.00	$200.00	$1,545.00
5		$1,145.00	$200.00	$200.00	$1,545.00
6		$1,145.00	$200.00	$200.00	$1,545.00
7		$480.77	$864.23	$200.00	$1,545.00
8			$1,345.00	$200.00	$1,545.00
9			$1,345.00	$200.00	$1,545.00
10			$1,345.00	$200.00	$1,545.00
11			$1,345.00	$200.00	$1,545.00
12			$1,345.00	$200.00	$1,545.00
13			$786.96	$758.04	$1,545.00
14				$1,545.00	$1,545.00
15				$1,545.00	$1,545.00
16				$1,545.00	$1,545.00
17				$1,545.00	$1,545.00
18				$1,486.11	$1,486.11

This method would save you $11,196 in interest charges. Both methods have you paying off all of your debts in 18 months, but you'll save an additional $613 following the Avalanche method. The Avalanche method is mathematically better than the Snowball method. We can hear you saying already, "well if the debt avalanche method is the best strategy to save money and time, then why bother with the snowball method?" With the debt snowball method, you feel the progress that much sooner as you'll be able to pay off your first debt completely in potentially only a few months. The debt avalanche will not work as effectively if you lose motivation. Just like with your home loan, it's important not to discount the impact psychology plays and having small wins that can keep you motivated.

Ultimately, the best method is the one you can stick to. If you are a person that is energised by saving the most amount of money, go with Avalanche, but if you need more motivation to pay off debt, then go with the debt snowball method. Whatever option you go with, the key is to focus your extra repayments on one debt at a time.

What if your debts will take much longer, and you expect it will be years before you can pay them off. You may feel like you're struggling because it seems as though your whole paycheck, is just paying off these loans and you aren't able to do anything that you enjoy and no method feels as though it will motivate you.

If you have completed a Living Budget from the previous chapter and are unable to allocate any money for yourself, consider paying off your first loan using the snowball method to get an early win, then reward yourself with a small regular amount. So if you were putting $100 a week towards your first debt, once it's paid off, keep $20 a week for yourself and use the remaining towards the debt snowball method. Even if it's just enough to be able to enjoy some small luxuries such as a couple of coffees. Make sure you have some money going into your Splurge account. Each time you reach a milestone of paying off a debt, celebrate a little by repeating the process of allocating some back to yourself and your splurge account. Being able to increase this will help motivate you as it will increase your sense of freedom in more ways than one.

The key is to make sure that you continue to spend within your limits as you progress with your goals. Each time you can reward yourself by allocating yourself a little bit more spending money to have a touch more freedom as you get your life back together. This will also help to keep you motivated by rewarding you for the achievements that you've been making and getting your financial life back on track. Once you have this sorted, you can go back to living life on your own terms rather than having bad debt hanging over you.

So what about things like balance transfers with credit card and interest-free deals.

If you have multiple credit cards, you are probably currently paying somewhere between 17% - 24% interest on these loans. If you can get approved for a balance transfer deal consider taking the opportunity but make sure that the credit card that you just paid off gets chopped up and closed down and is to never, ever be touched again.

When you get your new credit card, the moment it arrives, do the same. Chop the damn thing up. You do not want to spend on this credit card. The whole point is to pay it off. Don't be adding new expenses.

If your only debt other than your home loan is a single credit card debt that you wish to refinance to an interest free balance transfer promotion. Just remember that interest-free deals only last for a short period of time before returning to the high interest rate levels that you are trying to escape. Make sure that you take the interest free period into account with the aim of paying it off in time. Even aim to finish a month or two early if you can and close off the account as soon as the amount is zero.

It's also important to be aware that each time you apply for a credit card it does get noted on your credit rating and applying for cards on a frequent basis may have a negative impact later on such as when applying for or refinancing a home loan.

So, what if your debt problem means you are not coping. Sometimes people get themselves into trouble, by making poor choices or following the poor choices of others, into situations that they feel that there is no escape from. If this is you, please seek professional help. If you feel that you aren't coping, then we strongly urge you to get in contact with an organisation such as Lifeline on 13 11 44.

Another great resource is the National Debt Helpline. It's a not-for-profit service that helps people in Australia tackle their debt problems.

They are not a lender and don't 'sell' anything or make money from you. Their professional financial counsellors offer a free, independent and confidential service. If you need to reach out, please call them on 1800 007 007 or visit the website www.ndh.org.au

CHAPTER 10

GET AHEAD

$ $ $

Sometimes the wage that you earn from your regular 9-to-5 job simply doesn't go far enough. So you've completed the Spending Plan exercise, yet you don't have enough left over to help you reach your other goals after covering your basic living expenses or you have some ambitious goals to smash out some debt. You may need another way to earn some more money to help you get ahead.

You need wiggle room in your Spending Plan whether it is to help get you out of debt, to invest, or to simply allow you to enjoy the things you want and value. So, what can you do if your wage is already fully committed? Well, you can check out our chapter on how to ask for a pay raise. But if you've already done that and you're still looking at ways to boost your income and make the most of the money you have, then read on. We have taken some time to look into things that you can do, that everybody can do, to make some more money.

It doesn't have to be forever but sometimes you do need to earn some money on top of your regular job. You may need extra income to set up your emergency fund. You might just be starting your career in a low paid entry level position, or perhaps you are separating from your partner and starting all over again. Maybe you have a personal loan or credit card debt and paying it off is all it will take to improve your cash flow and get your Spending Plan in great shape.

Whatever the reason, knowing you need an income boost for a period of time is not a bad thing. Both Katherine and Amber have undertaken side hustles at different stages. Amber has cleaned commercial offices on the weekend to help make ends meet. Katherine had major pantry envy, so decided that the best way to get her dream Tupperware pantry was to do party planning for a few months. Not only did this mean earning extra cash, but it meant getting the items she wanted at wholesale rates. Boom!

If you know (or suspect) that you aren't earning enough to continue to live the way you want to, the worst thing you can do is, to do nothing. Denial is not your friend. It's time to get creative and get busy earning a little more.

First of all, even if you are working full time, you still have time to earn some more money. Unless you work 16 hours a day / 7 days a week. If it's important, you can find some time.

There are 168 hours in the week. If you are working fulltime at 40 hours a week, that still leaves you with 128 hours a week. Let's take out 56 hours (8 hours a night) for sleeping and you have 72 hours a week where you can be productive. Yes, you definitely need down time and time with friends and to enjoy yourself. However if you are prepared to use some of this time to make a little extra cash, what can you do....

To narrow it down, start by thinking a little bit creatively about what you do, what you're good at, how much time you have and think about ways that you can use that to generate some more cash for yourself. If you find yourself regularly being asked by friends or family to help out with a certain task, that's a great place to start.

If you want to see a range of odd jobs that are needed in your area, a great place to check out is **AirTasker** (www.Airtasker.com) It's an online platform where people put jobs up that they want other people to do for them. They list what the job is and how much they're willing to pay somebody else to do it. The most popular job on Airtasker by far is assembling IKEA furniture. Now I am horrible at putting together IKEA furniture. I once somehow managed to put an IKEA kids chair together almost backwards. Try to imagine what it would look like if Picasso had painted an IKEA child's chair… yep it looked like that. Some might say it was beautiful, but unfortunately my husband is not amongst them and I have since been banned from assembling flat pack furniture. But there will be some of you reading this book that are great at it and may even enjoy the satisfaction or challenge of putting the items together. If you wanted to earn some extra money, this would be a simple and easy solution. Other common tasks on Airtasker include gardening and cleaning. So jump on and see what tasks are available in your area.

Other well known options are driving services like **Uber/ Uber-eats**: I have a friend whose wife is on maternity leave at the moment and their household finances were quite tight. Five nights a week he goes out after their family dinner and drives an uber until he earns $50. Once he earns $50, he comes home. Now this $50 is his spending money and the money he uses to do whatever he wants. For a couple of hours in the evenings he makes $250 a week. He would not have this money otherwise and it means that he can then use his extra cash to go to the football, take his wife out for dinner, whatever he wants. This was serious money. If he doesn't feel like it, he doesn't go out and he doesn't earn the money that week. Unlike picking up a more official/traditional second job, it's an option that gives you the ability to earn extra cash and the flexibility to work the hours you want when you want and only if you want.

If you want something with a little more structure, we suggest having a look at doing something where you can earn penalty rates, so you get more money for your time. If you want to pick up something like stacking shelves at your local supermarket, do it on a Sunday. You can earn more money doing that then stacking shelves on another day of the week.

Perhaps you have a creative talent that can be converted into a **paid hobby**? We have a friend who excelled at crafts and sewing. This was a creative outlet for her, but she also needed to earn some extra money. She was a stay at home mum and needed something with minimum start-up costs that would be flexible by allowing her to work around her family's schedule. She ended up going to op shops and finding beautiful vintage buttons on pieces of clothing that she uses to make into beautiful earrings. She sells these for about $20 a set and is making good money. She has time to go to the store and hunt out buttons and sells them online. She has a Facebook group where she displays and sells her creative pieces and also has a local market stall. If you have an artistic or creative side, or love the idea of upcycling something, why not give it a go?

If you would prefer to go with something more structured, you may also think about **direct marketing companies**, such as Tupperware. Both of us while on maternity leave decided to give selling Tupperware a go. It got us out of the house and I felt like we were doing something productive in a social setting. It was also a good money earner. As mentioned earlier it also meant that we could buy items at wholesale prices. Even if you've never been in a sales job before, selling a product that you love makes it that much easier. There are lots of these types of companies around. Everything from linen, to beauty products, to candles or even Thermomixers. The trick is to find one that you honestly like and give it a go. You usually get training and support and you can make some real money to add into your Spending Plan or purchase an item on your wish list at wholesale prices.

Having **unused space** is also a great way to earn extra money. If you live in an area where car parking fees are high and you have an unused parking space such as your driveway or allocated parking in your apartment building, look into the possibility of whether you can rent this space. The same goes for your home. If you have a spare bedroom and are open to the idea of living with another person, whether it's a longer term arrangement or a short term paid cultural exchange placement. This can provide a valuable additional source of income with minimal or no impact on your time.

Another way to get a boost to your wallet is to **sell things you no longer need**. We all end up with an accumulation of stuff in our life and if you take the time to go through it, you'll find things in there that are valuable and that you can sell to make money. Do you really need that old Play Station? Are you really ever going to use that gym set again? Are you really going to ever wear that dress again? Take the time to consider what you have and what you need. It's also about priorities. Sell the extra things now to get out of debt, start an emergency fund or boost your investments.

If you don't like the idea of selling your items, **consider renting** them out. There are online services available that allow you to rent out items that you wish to retain, but you are likely to have periods of time where you don't need the item yourself. It could be a collection of designer dresses or handbags, a caravan, trailer or even your car. Make sure you check with your car insurer for rules and regulations that may apply before you jump into this.

Do you love to cook? There might be somebody at your work that gets serious food envy every time you bring your home-made lunch or snacks to work and they'd be willing to pay you to make their lunch or snacks. Perhaps you love to walk your dog everyday, but your neighbour struggles to find the time. You can offer a dog walking service to your neighbours, allowing you to earn money with barely any additional commitments on your time.

These are just a few ideas and we hope you feel inspired. If you really think about it, there are always plenty of ways to make money and do extra jobs. You might even find that what starts off as something extra to do becomes your full-time job. We challenge you to try something new. Have a go at making more money. This week try to do something that makes you an extra $50. Take that $50 and once you've built your emergency buffer, put it towards your goal and priorities and see how a little bit of effort can make a really big difference over time for your financial future.

CHAPTER 11

GET A GURU

$ $ $

Using the services of a professional adviser.

Not everyone needs a financial adviser. Not everyone needs a personal trainer either, but having one in your corner is likely to get you far better results. There are some similarities between the two and both are there to guide you and keep you accountable to your goals. While they can help you, it's you who will have to do the heavy lifting. They can't do it for you. You get the picture.

There are some key milestones in life where seeking the services of an adviser can save you from making a costly mistake, or help your money go further and therefore reach your goals. They have knowledge and experience to help you navigate areas that can be constantly changing such as superannuation and other areas such as insurance and investing.

You may just wish to see an adviser for a financial health check or a one-off piece of advice, or you may want to have one on retainer so you can check in with them regularly.

But how do you find one you can trust? You don't have to ask too many people whether they know a good financial adviser before you will hear someone's horror story. My cousin's neighbour's, Aunty Jean went to a financial adviser who talked her into re-mortgaging her house and investing in a racing frog. The stupid thing couldn't hop to save itself and poor Jean, who should be enjoying her golden years has now had to move in with her daughter, whose son is the interstate yodelling champion, and she hasn't gotten a wink of sleep since.

Yep, there have been cases of dodgy advice, where advisers have placed their own interests ahead of their clients. The financial advice industry has undergone massive change from being a job you could simply walk into after going to a weekend course to now requiring a degree qualification and significant ongoing professional development each year. There are now laws in place that requires your interests to always be placed first and there are no longer commissions paid on investments and superannuation products. That doesn't mean that it's impossible to receive poor advice. Every industry has its rogues. There are court cases with doctors and lawyers who are sued for malpractice or negligence or who have breached their duty of care. However I still go and see my GP when I need some medical advice. The relationship works because I know my doctor, they know my history and understand me. The same goes for working with an adviser.

There are always times when it is tempting to try and figure it out all yourself online. We're all for improving your financial literacy or learning more about your health etc. But I try to avoid google doctor because it always seems to end up telling me that I may have cancer or am dying. Similarly googling financial advice won't make for a healthy bank account either.

There are lots of sources of advice to be found out in the real world. Many people will ask their friends and family before ever seeking a professional opinion. But if you are seeking a professional opinion, where should you go? What should you know to help you find the right help and be confident in your decision?

Let's start by looking at the different types of professionals you may work with and help you understand how they can help you along with a few tell-tale signs (good or bad) that you should be looking for and what you could expect when meeting with an adviser.

For most people, when they first get help, it's usually by completing the tax return and speaking to their accountant. Accountants can certainly help you maximise your tax return and can give you some guidance. At the end of the day they can't give you personal advice (other than so far as it relates to tax) unless they are actually licensed to do so. There are some accountants who are also licenced advisers, but they are few and far between. You're more likely to find a financial adviser who has an accounting degree, but who is not a practicing tax accountant.

You are also likely to seek help from other professionals such as mortgage brokers. They provide an invaluable service and can provide you with advice on your borrowing eligibility and guidance when it comes to your mortgage and finding you the best deal or home-loan product. But they are unable to offer personal financial advice. For example, they won't or can't take into account your future financial goals, such as having children and sending them to private school. They can help you figure out how much you can borrow for a house based on your current circumstances, but that's it. In short, they can tell you what you *can* do but not what you *should* do.

Red Flag on Property: It's really important to know that because of the nature of property, it's not an area that's regulated when it comes to giving and receiving advice. Whilst there are some really valuable property related services available such as buyers' agents and the like, it can also be like swimming in the open ocean in shark infested waters while sporting an open wound. Australians have a love affair with property and it's a great way to invest for many people.

However, too many times to count, I have seen people being cold called or invited to seminars where they tell you there is a new way to be able to invest in property by legally using the part of your wage that your employer sets aside for tax, so it will cost you very little and in 10 years you'll be financially set for life. These seminars are often linked up with property developers and for each property they sell you they stand to earn either side of $30,000 in commission, and they'll tell you all of the positives, but none of the drawbacks.

To ensure you commit, they'll also organise your mortgage, and sometimes even try to convince you to double down by setting up a Self Managed Super Fund and buying more properties through your super. There's usually a lot of pressure and push to show you how little it will cost you to invest by using depreciation schedules, without telling you the impact this will have the day you sell the property. But the moment interest rates rise, your wages takes a hit, or you lose a tenant you can find yourself scrambling to service hundreds of thousands or more than a million dollars worth of debt. There is little or no duty-of-care requirement to you in these scenarios and massive conflicts of interest.

Please don't get us wrong. We think property is a great investment option, but we want you to understand that if you're being sold a property via a seminar or what started off as an unsolicited call, then just remember, their only aim is to sell you a property and there is no consideration about whether or not this is appropriate for you and your situation. If you receive one of these unsolicited calls, please KNOW 'today is NOT your lucky day' and you should hang up faster than a character is killed at a *Game of Thrones* wedding.

If you want someone who is going to look at your individual circumstances and work out what the best path forward is for you specifically, you will need to see a financial adviser. Financial advisers and financial planners are one in the same thing. These are actually licensed and protected terms. If you see someone calling themselves a financial strategist or wealth coach, tread with extreme caution! In most cases, (but not all cases) this is someone giving advice, who doesn't have a license to do so.

So why should you see a licensed financial adviser? In short, they have a legal requirement to act in your best interest. This gives you protection. Every financial adviser must be licensed through the Australian Securities and Investments Commission (ASIC) and meet specific educational requirements. That doesn't mean that if you go to three different advisers, you will get the same answers from each. There is rarely a "best" solution. So how do you identify an adviser who is going to be a good fit for you?

Start by asking for recommendations from people you know and trust. If you don't have any recommendations from people that you know personally, there are a few places online worth a look. The Adviser Ratings website (www.adviserratings.com.au) lists every registered financial adviser in Australia and includes feedback and ratings from their clients. This is a good way to find an adviser in your area and to get an idea of what kind of services they may offer, as advisers can often have a niche such as specialising in people who are preparing to retire, while others specialise in superannuation, investing, budgeting and cash flow advice. The Adviser Ratings website will also tell you whether they offer a free initial meeting and the likely cost of the services.

So why would you see a financial adviser? It's the same reason you would see a personal trainer for your physical fitness. You already know exercise is important, but if you want to get to your peak physical fitness, or simply need to have someone to keep you accountable, they will be there to help you.

A financial adviser's role can be summarised as achieving 6 key areas:

- save you money
- make you money
- save you time and/or provide convenience
- protect your financial health
- pay you money
- improve your financial knowledge and understanding

A financial adviser can also help adjust your plan as your circumstances change.

Seeing a financial adviser comes with a cost. For every hour that you spend with a financial adviser, there is another three to four hours worth of work behind the scenes. So not only are you paying for the time that you spend with them, you are also paying for the level of work required in the background.

It's similar to going out for dinner at a restaurant. You don't just pay for the ingredients of the meal, you are paying for the time it took to prepare those ingredients, the staff employed to serve you such as the waiters and front of house staff, the chef's time preparing the meal on the night and their years of experience, as well as the rent of the building, the electricity costs, and for all the other running and licensing costs etc. When you go out for dinner, you don't consider these costs. But you are prepared to pay more for dinner out when you know the cost of preparing your own dinner at home would be far less. But unless you're a chef yourself, it's unlikely you'll be able to get the same results in the same amount of time.

So are you keen to see an adviser? You need to first find someone who can help you with your area of need. Some advisers will only deal with high net worth clients and business owners, whereas others focus on a particular niche and others are happy to provide advice regardless of the level of savings you have.

Reading this book will help you get your basic finances in order. Money is the tool that financial advisers work with, so an important step is making sure that not all of your paycheck is being spent on day-to-day expenses. You need to look after not only your current finances but your future financial self.

So what areas can a financial adviser help you with:

- Superannuation;
    - How much do you need to retire and assessing whether you are on track
    - Are you invested in the right option and is it performing well
    - Are the fees competitive
    - Help with consolidating multiple superannuation accounts
    - Maximising your contributions to help you pay less tax or take advantage of government incentives such as the co-contribution

- Debt & Cashflow
    - Helping you structure your Spending Plan and cashflow and keep you accountable to your saving goals

- ○ Helping you assess whether a salary packaging arrangement is worthwhile
- ○ Helping you to take advantage of government assistance programs such as the First Homeowner's Super Saver Scheme
- ○ Putting strategies in place to help you pay down your debts faster
- ○ Helping you determine how much you should borrow rather than how much you could when purchasing a property.

- Personal insurance
  - ○ Assessing the types and levels of cover you need based on the outcomes you want
  - ○ Advice on the ownership structure (via super, personally or a company etc)
  - ○ Advice on the features and options as well as recommending an insurer that suits you based on your occupation, medical history and hobbies
  - ○ Negotiating terms to get you the best outcome
  - ○ Help when you need to make a claim
  - ○ Taking you through the initial application process and keeping your policy up to date as the years go by.

- Creating and using your wealth
  - ○ How to best invest any savings whether it's starting an investment bond, using managed funds, shares, or cashflow advice around investing in property
  - ○ Helping you plan for life events such as saving for a wedding, planning parental leave and preparing to retire etc
  - ○ Helping you to make smart decisions and avoid bad ones such as panic selling during a temporary market correction
  - ○ Advice on accessing aged care and assistance with Centrelink and government benefits.

To summarize, there are a million ways to provide strategies and advice to help you reach your goals and make the most of your money.

There are many more examples, but the above gives you a good idea. Some areas are purely strategic advice, whereas other areas will require you to make changes to your providers whether it is an insurance, super or investment provider.

So what's typically involved when it comes to meeting with an adviser for the first time? Before you receive any advice, you legally need to receive what is called a Financial Services Guide, commonly referred to as an FSG. It has plenty of information (which can be a bit dry), but in short it tells you the details of your adviser, whom they are licensed through, what kind of advice and services they can provide, how much you can likely expect to pay for the adviser's services, and what to do in the event that you have a complaint.

Either at or prior to your first meeting you'd generally be expected to provide information about yourself from basic contact details, through to details about your income, expenses, assets and liabilities and what outcomes you hope to get out of seeking advice.

Be prepared: if you are using an adviser to get personal insurances, your conversations are about to go a whole lot deeper than 'meeting someone you know on your daily public commute' *polite* to 'the confessions of a drunk girl crying in the nightclub bathroom at 1 AM' *explicit*. They need to ask you some very personal questions. So make sure you are ready to share the requisite personal info you would rather not tell your mother.

Some advisers will offer a free initial meeting, but this is becoming less common. You can usually still access an initial phone meeting at the adviser's expense. The free initial meeting is slowly fading out with the drive to higher levels of professionalism. Just as you would expect a physiotherapist, doctor, lawyer or accountant to charge you for an initial consult, this is becoming more and more the norm in financial advice.

Following your meeting, the adviser will need to research your current arrangements and spend time going through your current circumstances in detail. Your adviser will work out what you need to do to get to your future financial goals. This service can include making sure your Spending Plan is right, helping you with a debt reduction plan, organising personal insurances and growing your wealth. All this advice will take into account risks, opportunities, your personal situation and the type of service you need. From there you'd want to receive a Terms of Engagement or something in writing which sets out the scope of work they will undertake for you and the costs involved which has been tailored to your goals based on the estimated level of work involved and expertise required. It's important that you have a clear understanding of what services you will receive and what it will cost.

When you receive advice, it will be in writing in a document called a Statement of Advice. This document confirms your current situation, your reasons for seeking advice and then provides recommendations on what you should specifically do to meet those goals. It spells out the risks and benefits and the costs involved, including any fees and charges payable to your adviser. This document will be your roadmap to get to where you want to be in the future and keep ahead AND stay ahead.

Some of the advice will never involve a financial product, such as strategies around building an emergency fund, or paying down your debts, but often there is a financial product involved such as superannuation, investment options or insurance as these are the vehicle to getting some of your other strategies underway. When it comes to which products they recommend, an adviser is only allowed to provide advice on products that have been researched and approved by their licensee. Many licensees in Australia are owned by product providers such as the big banks. Some of these licensees may only sell their own products. But there also are plenty of privately owned licensees which have no in-house products and give their advisers much broader access to options that they feel are suitable to be offered.

Always take a cautious approach when it comes to an in-house or affiliated product. Even if the strategy is a good fit, the adviser could be limited to offering the in-house brand only or a very limited range of products, and there could be better alternatives out there, but they are restricted and cannot give you advice on what could potentially be a better fit. In short, if you are being recommended a product, and especially if it is an in-house private brand, you should be asking a lot of questions about why this is the most suitable option for you, and why other options weren't considered.

Fortunately, there is an easy way to be able to identify what limits your adviser is operating under. You can ask the adviser directly, and by referring to the FSG, which explains who the licensee is behind the advice.

The legal requirement that advisers act in your best interest means that they must provide advice that leaves you in a better financial situation, not the best possible financial situation. So make sure whoever is giving you advice is licenced and has a broad range of options available to them.

Also given you are reading this book, flick to the other chapters on finances and get the basics down yourself, the better the education you have around concepts such as super, tackling your debts, investing and your personal insurances, the more value you will get out of seeking advice and understand when you've found a good fit with an adviser whether it's a one-off piece of advice or an ongoing relationship.

EPILOGUE

$ $ $

Theres something so alluring about perfection. It shimmers like an oasis in the desert. Clearly visible, yet somehow also eternally unattainable. It's something our culture seems to focus on (especially in the age of social media). Some people earn a living promoting their image. Here is my perfect family and job and house and holiday. But it's bullshit. Like the Great and Powerful Oz, the image of perfection is just smoke and mirrors designed to impress people, while the truth is most of us have wonderful things happen to us and terrible things, and there are lots of mundane bits in the middle.

Perfection in your finances is also a bit of a furphy. We can all do better, and the problem with aiming for perfection is that sometimes it seems like such an overwhelming task that instead of doing something, people do nothing.

Change is hard. It takes time and commitment. So instead of perfection, let's aim for small and incremental changes. Being perfect is not the goal, changing and growing and being in a better financial position than you were this time last year, is the goal.

The truth is we gave up on perfection years ago. We know deep down that we have good intentions, but honestly, everything we do can be

improved upon (you should have seen the first draft of this book... our editor is a miracle worker!!!).

Our lives are messy and chaotic and full of laughing at the most inappropriate times. And honestly, that's the way we like it now. Our finances aren't perfect either, but we have gotten so much joy out of the process of changing and getting better at this stuff, we wouldn't want it any other way. We are proud of the growth in ourselves as we tackled our finances and that's what we want for you too.

If you are interested in hearing more about our financial journey, we have a weekly podcast where we talk more about our own struggles and triumphs. Search Money Madams on your favourite podcast provider or find us here: https://moneymadams.libsyn.com/

You can also find out more of what we are up to and access resources to help get you started on your own Money Madam journey on: https://moneymadams.com/ or follow us on FaceBook or Instagram.

ACKNOWLEDGEMENTS

$ $ $

Amber

Writing this book was about you, the reader. We want women to prosper and be empowered and have the financial security to be and do whatever is deep within their hearts to achieve.

But it would not have been possible without the love and support and encouragement of many people. Thank you, Jenni Walke, for helping us clarify who we are and what we wanted to give to the world.

Thank you to the beautiful friends who listened endlessly to the book progress updates and said with all the conviction in the world "How many copies do you need me to buy?" I appreciate you more than you know Emily Radburn, Tanya Singh, Sally Winton, Tara Hawke, Amy Clement, Bernadette Esplin, Erika Heywood, Liz Mcauliffe, Holly Hawke, Katie Diou, Karina Keast, Oriana Mamone and Deb Langford. I have never leaned so heavily on my tribe as I have during the time of writing this book and I am so grateful that you were there to hold me up and carry me through. Thank you.

My Dad, who seemed not the least bit surprised at all that I was writing a book.

My dear friend, business partner and inspiration Katherine. I worked hard just to keep up with you. You are one of the hardest working, smartest people I know and this journey has been a joy (almost all the time) because you have been beside me every step of the way.

My husband who put the children to bed while I was writing, folded washing and loved and supported me more than I thought was humanly possible. I adore you. Thank you, Rowan.

To Tilly and Scarly, all this is for you.

Amber

Katherine

Wring this book for me was a labour of love, with a small emphasis on the labour. By the time we were close to the end, like most pregnancies, I just wanted it out

In all seriousness, the idea of writing this book was born from our need to find a good reason to spend more time together in our increasingly busy lives which we nicknamed our whine and wine catch-ups. The idea of writing this book started as a tiny seed over 10 years ago and never would have been realised if it wasn't for the amazing people who encouraged us along the way.

To Peter who first told me that I had something worth saying, and when I told him that there was nothing I could say that hadn't already been said, pointed out that people still needed to hear it from me as I had something special to offer.

To my clients whom I have helped over the years who have helped me by sharing their life journeys and ultimately increased my passion for the work I do each day. A shout out to Karen, whose own life journey inspires me when life gets tough and for being the inspiration behind some of the stories I share as life lessons.

Thank you to Brian who offered to build our website and his team members Andi and Cynthia who have been amazing supports and kept me sane.

Thank you to the team at Synchron who have always been like a second family to me. A special mention for Jack for agreeing to be the voice of the Money Madams podcast disclaimer and of course the compliance team who I still can't believe signed off on the disclosures we came up with.

A massive thank you to Amber, even though we aren't related you've always felt like a sister to me. You crack me up with your humour and sharp wit and amaze me with your wisdom and insight. There is no way

I could have done any of this without you. Thank you for being such an amazing friend and support, being your friend brings joy to my life, and whilst I'll probably always prefer red wine over white, you've convinced me Gin has its merits.

To my three boys, Zane, Aiden and Diesel who entertain and cheer me on with their 'dabs' and boasts that their mum is famous because they've seen her podcast cover on Google Home. Thank you for being my personal cheer squad. I love you and can't help but write it here even if it's not 'cool' to do so.

This book is about helping women to lead a life where they feel confident, supported and empowered. To know that it's okay to talk about money, without shame and to even have fun in doing so. We want to encourage all women who read this book to change the money conversation in Australia. Once that happens, financial literacy can be the gift they give to their own families and communities.

Lastly, thank you to you for reading this book, we hope you enjoyed reading it and learned something along the way.

Katherine

LIVING BUDGET
TEMPLATE

$ $ $

If you have always struggled to find a decent spreadsheet to help you budget, we have the answer!

We have built for you a spreadsheet that matches the principles we teach in this book. The first key is to take action on making changes and that starts with using a budget that will help you automate your cashflow. Our Living Budget template is super easy to use. With a single click, you can hide any unused income or expenses, so you only see what matters to you.

Our budget also allows you to include a second Splurge account based on whether you run your finances solo or wish to design a budget with your partner in mind. Once again, all with the single click of a button.

No matter whether you budget weekly, monthly or fortnightly, our template will convert and automatically work out your spending and income amounts for you based on your prefered frequency.

So what are you waiting for? It's time to start living your best life and automate your budget!

Find our Living Budget Template at: www.moneymadams.com/shop

THE MONEY MADAMS AS SPEAKERS AT YOUR NEXT EVENT

$ $ $

A mber Parr and Katherine Hayes have co-authored "Make Money Your B!tch"

They have helped hundreds of women increase their financial literacy and get on top of their money.

Katherine is a multi-award-winning financial advisor and Amber has been on her own financial journey, making their presentations both informative and entertaining.

They also produce a weekly podcast that covers topics such as money and relationships, budgeting basics and personal insurance. You can find their podcast called "Money Madams" on your favourite podcast platform or at www.moneymadams.com/blog

The Money Madams have written articles and have spoken at many events as well as conducting workshops. Their unique style of presentation ensures that their audiences receive valuable information they can take with them to be inspired and equipped to get their finances in order whilst having a great time.

Contact the Money Madams at www.moneymadams.com
connect@moneymadams.com

DO YOU WANT HELP DIRECTLY FROM ONE OF THE MONEY MADAMS?

$ $ $

Katherine Hayes is a fully qualified financial adviser who specializes in helping everyday Australians to secure their financial futures.

Katherine loves to help her clients put protection plans in place that they know they can rely on. Katherine makes sure they get the support and understanding they need not only when helping clients choose the types and levels of cover they need, but also by providing support at claim time.

This book can only provide general concepts on what you may wish to consider. If you would like Katherine to provide you with advice tailored to you personally (not to mention remove the stress of navigating the process alone) Katherine would love to help you sort out your finances, including your personal insurances. You can reach out to her and her team at service@hcis.com.au

You can find her website for Hayes & Co Insurance Services at www.hcis.com.au While Katherine and her business is based in Canberra, she is happy to offer appointments via Zoom.

ABOUT THE AUTHORS

$ $ $

Katherine Hayes

Katherine is a multi-award winning financial advisor based in Canberra with over 15 years industry experience. Before she settled down, she was a croupier sailing the high seas in the Caribbean, seeking fun and adventure.

Katherine is a mum to 3 crazy boys and a business owner.

Katherine brings her knowledge of personal finance strategies (after all she's a finance nerd at heart) combined with her kind approach that empowers others to lead their best Money Madams life.

Amber Parr

After studying to obtain a Bachelor of Arts (Communication Studies) Amber has spent almost 20 years in the public service.

She has taken the leap to go after her passion; using her dynamic, insightful and fun communication style to empower women to reach their financial dreams after undergoing her own personal financial journey.

Amber is a mum to two young girls and in her spare time (ha!) likes to...... well, she can't entirely remember but thinks she used to like movies and going to brunch with friends.